Editor: Katie Puckett
Designer: John Jamieson
Managing editor: Miranda Smith

Activity illustrations: Gina Suter
Additional designer: Joanne Brown
Cover designer: Poppy Jenkins
DTP coordinator: Nicky Studdart
Production controller: Eliot Sedman
Artwork archivists: Wendy Allison, Steve Robinson
Indexer: Rebecca Fairley

KINGFISHER
a Houghton Mifflin Company imprint
222 Berkeley Street
Boston, Massachusetts 02116
www.houghtonmifflinbooks.com

First published in 1999
First published in this format in 2005
10 9 8 7 6 5 4 3 2 1

1TR/0705/TIMS/BESTSET(RAINBOW)/128MA

LIBRARY OF CONGRESS CATALOGING-IN-PUBLICATION DATA
has been applied for.

ISBN 0-7534-5931-0
ISBN 978-07534-5931-7

Printed in China

My world of
Discovery

KINGFISHER
BOSTON

Contents

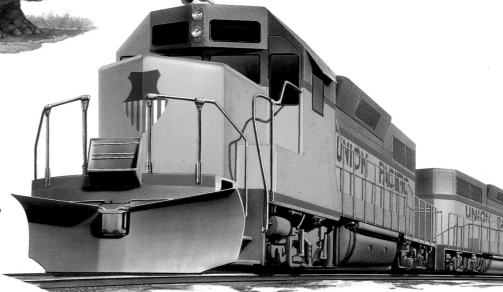

The Universe

The Universe

Everything that exists is part of the Universe. The Earth is in the Universe, and so are the Sun, the Moon, and everything else out in space. The Universe is enormous. No one knows how big it is, or where it begins and ends.

Some red giants grow into huge supergiants.

The Universe is made up of billions of stars. Stars are huge balls of burning gases. New stars are born all the time from clouds of dust and gas. Old stars fade and grow cold.

A star shines for billions of years.

Then it swells up into a big star called a red giant.

The outer layers of the star may escape into space.

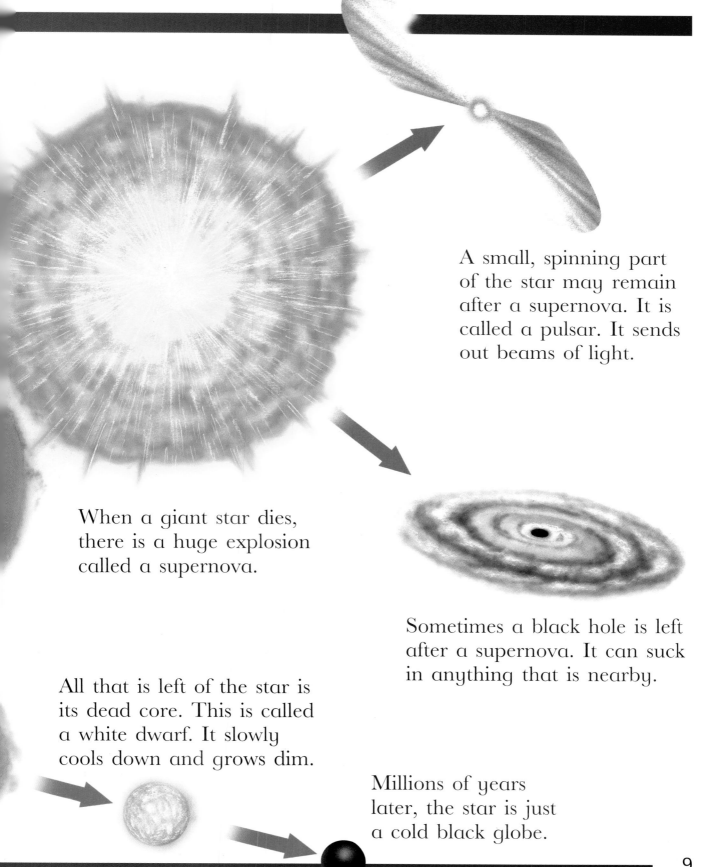

A small, spinning part of the star may remain after a supernova. It is called a pulsar. It sends out beams of light.

When a giant star dies, there is a huge explosion called a supernova.

Sometimes a black hole is left after a supernova. It can suck in anything that is nearby.

All that is left of the star is its dead core. This is called a white dwarf. It slowly cools down and grows dim.

Millions of years later, the star is just a cold black globe.

Night sky

On a clear night you can see that the sky is full of stars. Many of them form patterns in the sky called constellations. Long ago, people gave constellations names to make it easier to recognize them.

Astronomers use telescopes to look more closely at the stars and to see farther into space.

People in the northern part of the world see the stars shown here in the sky at night.

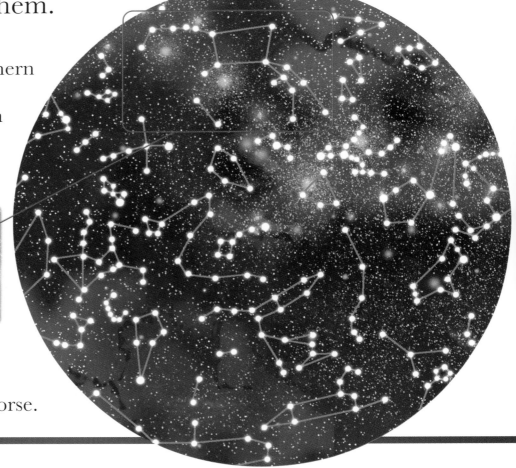

This constellation is named Pegasus, after a mythical horse.

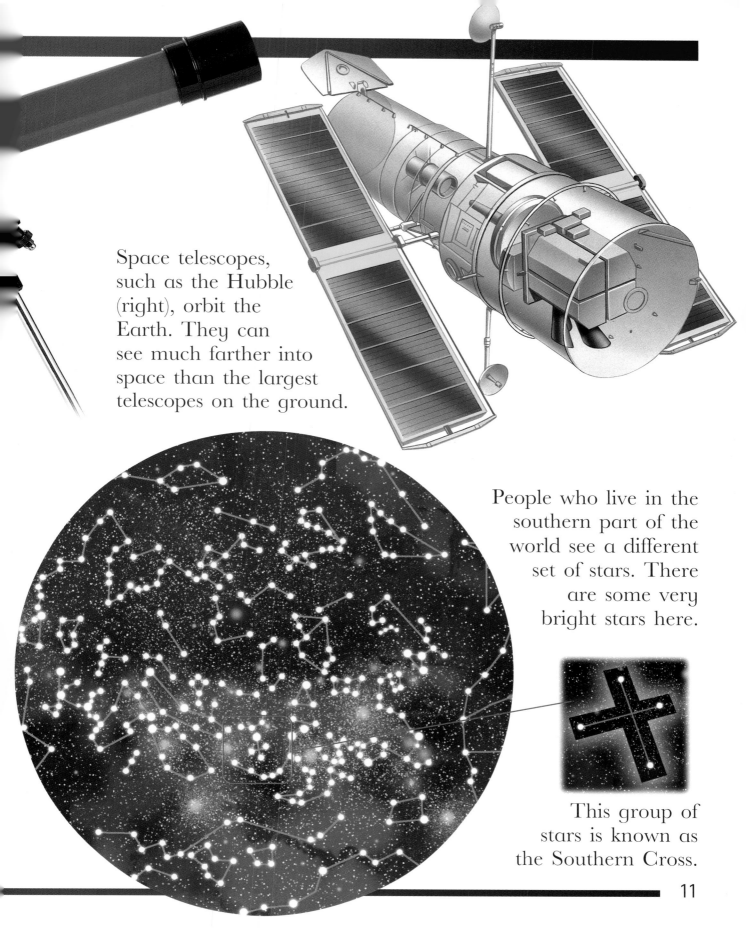

Space telescopes, such as the Hubble (right), orbit the Earth. They can see much farther into space than the largest telescopes on the ground.

People who live in the southern part of the world see a different set of stars. There are some very bright stars here.

This group of stars is known as the Southern Cross.

Galaxies

The Universe is made of gigantic groups of stars, called galaxies. There are billions of stars in each galaxy. Our planet Earth and the Sun are near the edge of a galaxy called the Milky Way.

If you look at the sky on a clear night, you may see a faint band of stars. This is part of the Milky Way. Our galaxy is a giant spiral of stars, slowly moving around a large group of stars in the middle.

The central part of a galaxy is called the nucleus

GALAXY PICTURE

Draw a spiral galaxy with glue on a big piece of black construction paper. Sprinkle glitter over the glue. Tilt the paper up to shake off any loose glitter.

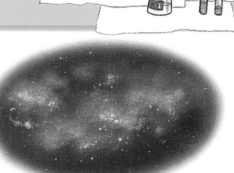

New stars form from areas of gas and dust

Galaxies are different shapes and sizes. These are the three main types.

Irregular-shaped galaxy

Egg-shaped galaxy

Spiral galaxy

The Solar System

A family of planets, moons, comets, and other chunks of rock is constantly spinning around the Sun. This family is called the Solar System. There are nine planets in the Solar System. They are made of rock, liquid, metal, or gas.

The planets in the Solar System are millions of miles apart. They are very different from each other. Mercury is the closest planet to the Sun and Pluto is the farthest away. Jupiter is the largest planet. It is so big that all the other planets could fit inside it together.

Jupiter

Mercury

Venus

Earth

Mars

14

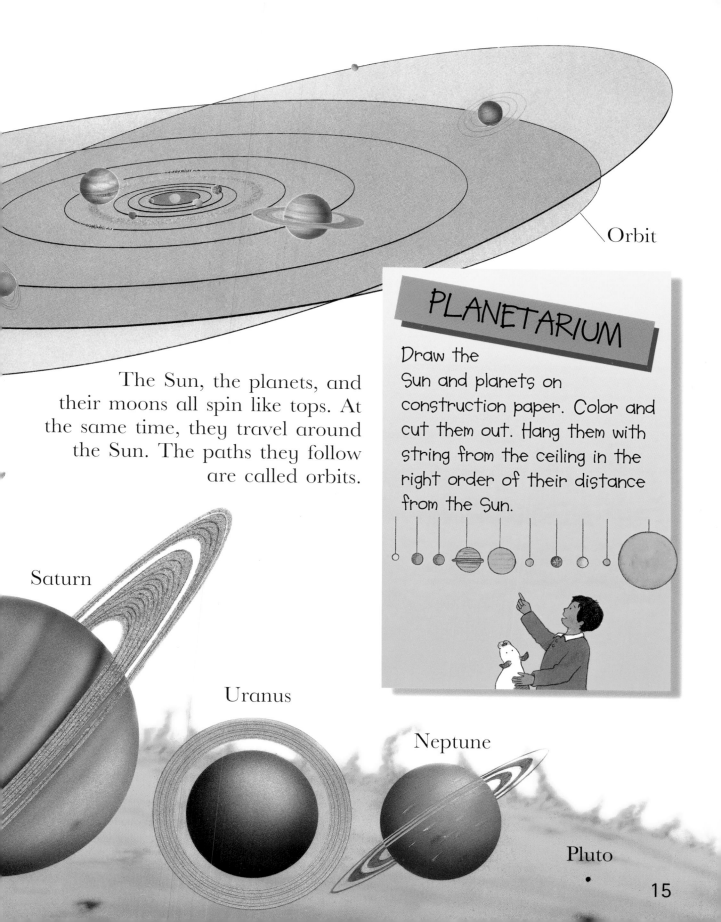

Orbit

The Sun, the planets, and their moons all spin like tops. At the same time, they travel around the Sun. The paths they follow are called orbits.

PLANETARIUM

Draw the Sun and planets on construction paper. Color and cut them out. Hang them with string from the ceiling in the right order of their distance from the Sun.

Saturn

Uranus

Neptune

Pluto

The Sun

The Sun is a star, just like the other stars you see in the sky at night. It is an enormous ball of burning gases, millions of times bigger than the Earth. The Sun gives off heat and light. Without it, the Earth would be cold, dark, and lifeless.

The Sun's rays can damage your skin if you spend too long outside on a sunny day. People use special creams to protect their skin.

Sun

The Earth is the third planet from the Sun. It travels around it at a distance of about 93 million miles. The Earth moves very fast, but it still takes a year (365 days) for it to complete its orbit.

Earth

The Sun is made mainly of a gas called hydrogen. The hottest part of the Sun is its core. Hot gases bubble up to the surface. They form a halo of gases called the corona. The dark patches on the surface of the Sun are sunspots. They are less hot than the rest of its surface.

Flaming jets of gas can flare up from the surface of the Sun.

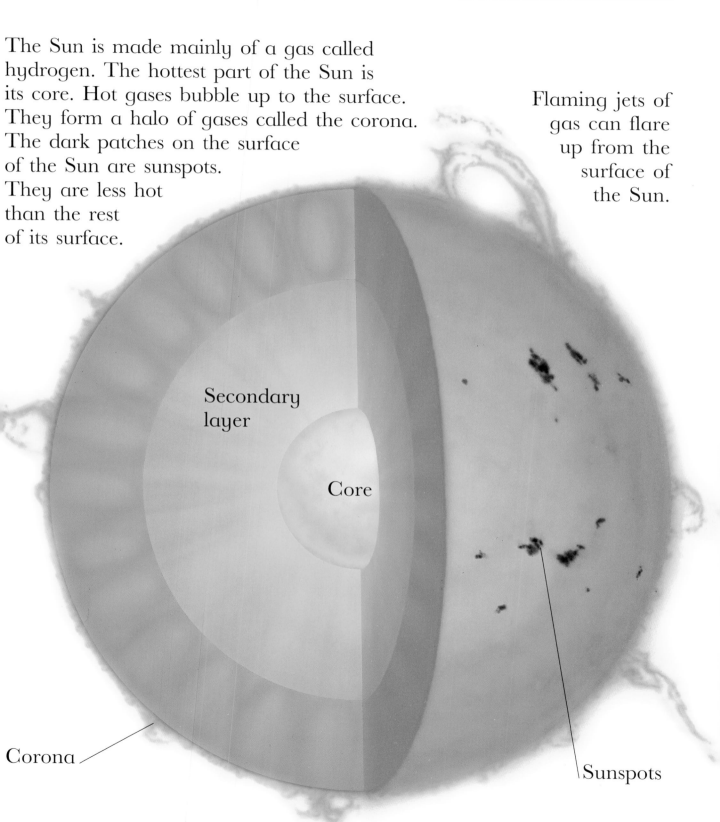

Secondary layer

Core

Corona

Sunspots

Close to the Sun

Mercury and Venus are the two planets in the Solar System closest to the Sun. They are both much, much hotter than the Earth. There are no signs of water on either planet. Nothing can grow or live on them.

Mercury spins very slowly, but it races around the Sun. It is burning hot on the side facing the Sun and icy cold on the other side.

Mercury is bare and rocky. On the surface it looks a lot like our Moon. It is covered with hills and giant hollows called craters.

Venus is about the same size as the Earth. It is the hottest planet of all. Its surface is covered by thick clouds of poisonous gases. These trap heat from the Sun.

You can often see Venus shining brightly in the sky just after sunset or before sunrise. It always looks as if it is very close to the Sun.

The surface of Venus is almost all flat, but there are a lot of old volcanoes, and raised areas of the lava that has flowed from them. Scientists think some of the volcanoes may still erupt from time to time.

19

The Earth

The Earth is the planet on which we live. It is a huge ball of rock spinning in space. The Earth is the only planet with water on it, and air for plants and animals to breathe. This is why there is life on Earth, but not on any other planet.

This is what the Earth looks like from space. Most of its surface is covered with water. The brown and green areas are land. The white patterns are clouds swirling in the sky.

It takes the Earth a day (24 hours) to spin once. It is day on the side of the Earth that faces the Sun. It is night on the side that faces away from it.

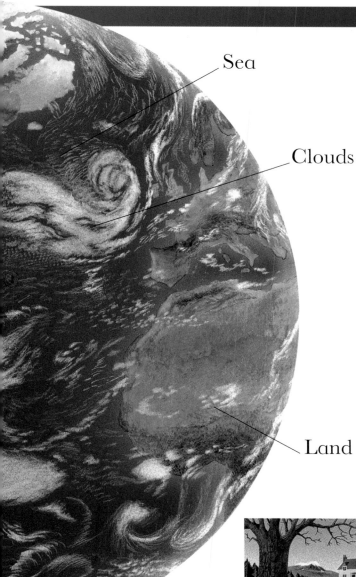

Sea

Clouds

Land

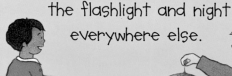

NIGHT AND DAY

Hold a globe and ask a friend to shine a flashlight at it. Make the globe spin. The flashlight is like the Sun. It is day in the area lit by the flashlight and night everywhere else.

Spring

Fall

The Earth spins at an angle, so the seasons change as the Earth moves around the Sun. It is summer in the part of the world that is closest to the Sun.

Summer

Winter

The Moon

The Moon is the closest object in space to us. It is a little over one-fourth the size of the Earth, and takes about a month to travel around it. The Moon has no air or water, so nothing can grow on it or live there.

The Moon turns as it orbits the Earth, so that the same side of it is always facing the Earth. The dark areas on the Moon are plains.

The surface of the Moon is rocky and dusty. There are thousands of craters. These were made millions of years ago when large rocks from space crashed into the Moon.

New moon

Half moon, first quarter

Full moon

Half moon, last quarter

Crescent waning

The Moon looks as if it changes shape. This is because we only see the part of it that is lit by the Sun. The sunlit part changes as the Moon moves around the Earth. Every month the Moon waxes (seems to grow bigger), then wanes (grows smaller).

MOON DIARY

Make a chart with a square for each day of the month. Draw what the moon looks like and describe it every night for a month.

Mars

Mars is the fourth planet from the Sun. It is the planet most like the Earth, but it is much colder because it is farther from the Sun. A day on Mars is about the same length as a day on Earth. Mars also has summer and winter seasons.

Mars is often called the Red Planet because its rocks are a rusty red color. Winds and storms blow reddish dust around, making Mars look pink from Earth.

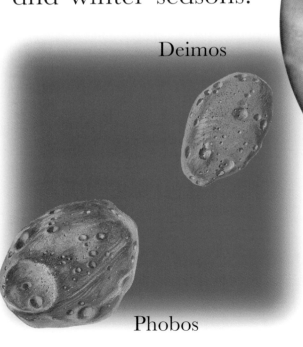

Deimos

Phobos

Mars is circled by two small, dark moons, called Phobos and Deimos. They are strangely shaped, a bit like lumpy potatoes.

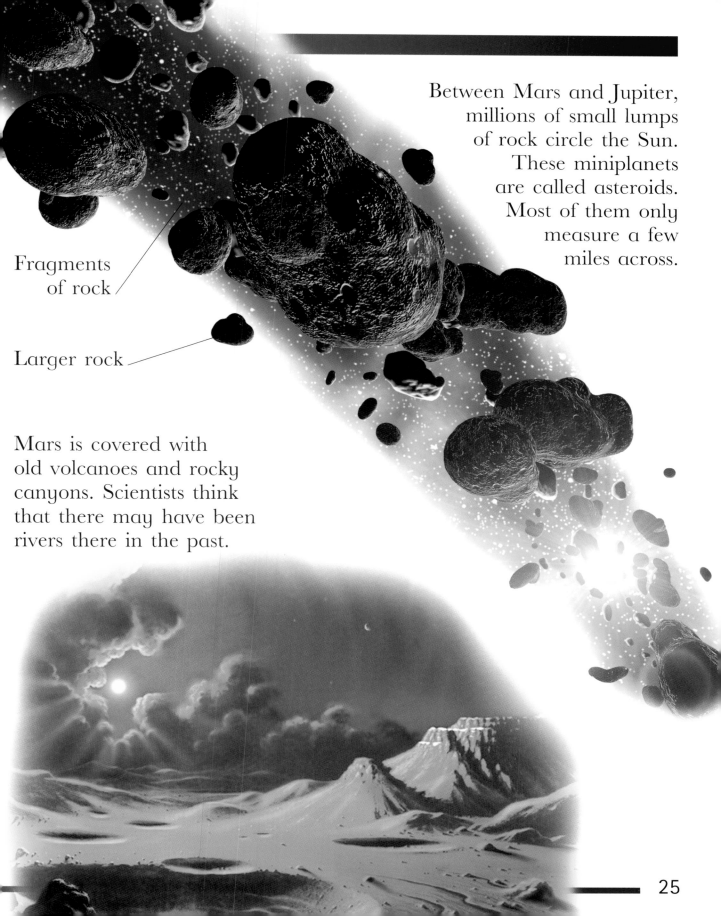

Between Mars and Jupiter, millions of small lumps of rock circle the Sun. These miniplanets are called asteroids. Most of them only measure a few miles across.

Fragments of rock

Larger rock

Mars is covered with old volcanoes and rocky canyons. Scientists think that there may have been rivers there in the past.

The giant planets

Beyond the asteroids are two enormous gas planets, Jupiter and Saturn. Both of them are circled by rings and moons. Jupiter is the largest planet in the Solar System, larger than all the others put together.

Icy cold clouds cover the surface of Jupiter. Strong winds blow these into bands of different colors.

Swirling clouds

Jupiter has 63 moons. One of them, Io, has active volcanoes on it. Io's rocky surface (left) is dyed red and orange by sulfur from its volcanoes.

Saturn is a spinning ball of gas and liquid. It is circled by at least 34 rocky moons. The planet's surface is covered in fast-moving clouds.

Icy rings

Strong winds race around Saturn

Saturn's rings are really thousands of narrow ringlets. They are made of millions of pieces of glittering ice. Most of these are small, but some measure several miles across.

MAKE JUPITER

Mix turpentine with drops of yellow and red oil paint. Put drops of color in a tray of water and swirl them around with a paintbrush. Lay a circle of paper on top. Lift it off and hang it up to dry.

Distant planets

Out near the edge of the Solar System there are three planets: Uranus, Neptune, and Pluto. They are so far away that they can't be seen with the naked eye. No space probe has visited Pluto, the most distant planet, so we do not know much about it.

Neptune is a bluish color. It has 13 moons. Triton, its largest moon, is the coldest object in the Solar System. Its cracked, frozen surface is dotted with volcanoes. These erupt with plumes of black dust and gases.

Pluto is the smallest planet of all. It has one moon, called Charon, which is half its size. Pluto follows an oval-shaped orbit around the Sun. This means that it is sometimes closer to the Sun than Neptune.

Uranus is four times bigger than the Earth. It is circled by 27 moons and about 11 narrow rings of small rocks.

Moving stars

You can see many things in the sky that are not stars or planets. Meteors and comets are burning lumps of rock that look like streaks of light whizzing across the sky.

Meteors are often called shooting stars. They are actually flecks of space dust which burn up in the air surrounding the Earth.

Lumps of space rock that crash into Earth are called meteorites. Even small ones like this make massive craters (left).

A comet hangs in the sky like a huge star with a tail. Comets are lumps of ice and rock that orbit the Sun. Their tails can be many millions of miles long.

Crumbling pieces of rock and ice

Nucleus

Jets of dust and gas

The Sun's heat melts the surface of the comet, making a cloud of gas and dust that blows into a giant tail.

The World Around Us

About our world

The Earth is amazingly varied. It has hot deserts, huge oceans, steamy rain forests, and frozen lands. Each part of the Earth has its own climate, or type of weather. The plants and animals adapt to where they live.

The landscape changes wherever you go. There are natural features, such as mountains. Landmarks such as oil wells have been made by people.

6

4

5

1

3

2

Most of our planet is covered by water. A thin blanket of air surrounds the Earth. Weather is produced by changes in this blanket of air.

1. Sea
2. River
3. Lake
4. Rain
5. Waterfall
6. Mountain
7. Forest
8. Oil well
9. Animals
10. City

Volcano

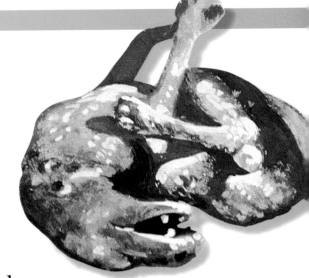

A volcano is a mountain that explodes. Deep below the surface of the Earth, the rocks are so hot that they melt. When a volcano erupts, this red-hot melted rock bursts out of a hole at the top of the mountain.

This dog was buried in the lava from a volcano in Pompeii, Italy, in A.D. 79.

ERUPTION!

Make a cone out of construction paper, leaving a hole at the top. Put a shallow plastic bowl in the hole. Add a little red powder paint and some baking soda. Carefully add some vinegar and watch the volcano erupt.

Hot, melted rock is called magma when it is under the ground, and lava when it reaches the surface.

During an eruption,
boiling lava pours
down the mountainsides,
destroying everything
in its path. The lava
cools slowly in the
air. Later, it
hardens into
new rock.

Earthquakes

The top layer of the Earth, the crust, is like a giant jigsaw puzzle. It is made up of huge, interlocking pieces that shift very slowly all the time. Sometimes they don't move smoothly and this makes the ground shake. It is an earthquake!

An earthquake is very frightening. The ground trembles and buildings can collapse, killing people. Earthquakes usually last only a few minutes but they can cause a lot of damage.

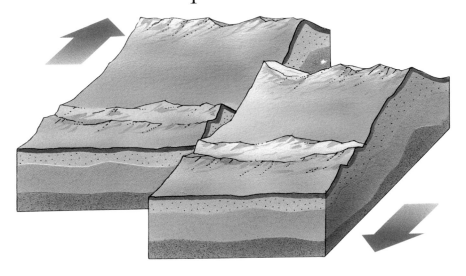

An earthquake happens when two pieces of the Earth's crust, or plates, try to move past each other and scrape together. They push and grind in opposite directions, making the rocks tilt and slip.

The shock waves from an earthquake can create giant waves called "tsunamis," which speed across the sea. They tower up when they reach land, destroying whole villages and towns.

Earthquakes may cause fires because underground fuel lines are broken.

Cracks large enough to swallow cars can open up in the ground.

Water cycle

The air is full of water vapor—tiny drops of water too small to see. Rain doesn't just come from the sky, but from the water that is all around us. The amount of water on Earth stays the same, but it keeps moving around.

The clouds grow heavier and are blown over the land.

Water vapor rises and forms clouds.

Water from the sea turns to water vapor.

As water is warmed by the Sun, it seems to dry up. In fact, it rises into the air as water vapor. As water vapor rises, it cools down and turns back into drops of water. These form clouds, and it rains.

If it is cold, it may snow rather than rain. The drops of water in the clouds freeze into ice crystals and these join together to make delicate snowflakes. No two snowflakes are ever the same.

Water in the clouds falls as rain, hail, sleet, or snow.

Rainwater runs into rivers and flows back into the sea.

MAKE A SNOW GLOBE

Find a jar with a tight lid. Glue small plastic toys inside the lid. Pour water into the jar until it is nearly full. Add some glitter and screw on the lid. Shake the jar and turn it upside down.

Life of a river

Many rivers start life in the mountains. Streams of rainwater run from high to low land. They join together and grow into a river that flows downhill toward the sea.

A river provides food for all kinds of creatures. There are many fish, such as this salmon.

Rain falls high in the mountains.

Streams run into each other.

Waterfall

A river changes at each stage of its journey. It starts life as a bubbling stream, but by the time it reaches the sea, it is wider and flows much more slowly.

The river grows wider

Reeds and rushes grow along a river.

When a river drops sharply downhill over steep ledges of rock, it makes waterfalls. These splash and make a lot of spray.

The river winds its way across the land

All rivers end in the sea. The place where a river flows into the sea is the mouth of the river.

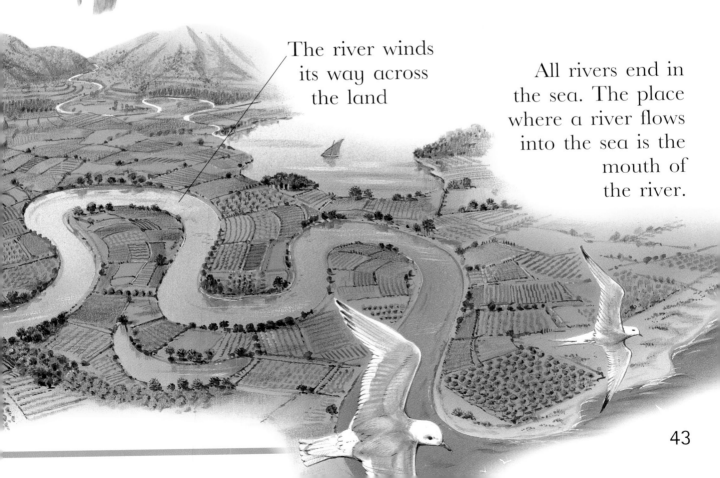

Saving our planet

Our planet faces many problems. The air and seas are getting polluted, or dirty, and some plants and animals are dying out. The Earth's natural fuels, such as gas, coal, and oil, are being used up.

Fumes from factories and cars pollute the air with chemicals. These dissolve in clouds and make acid rain, which harms wildlife and plants.

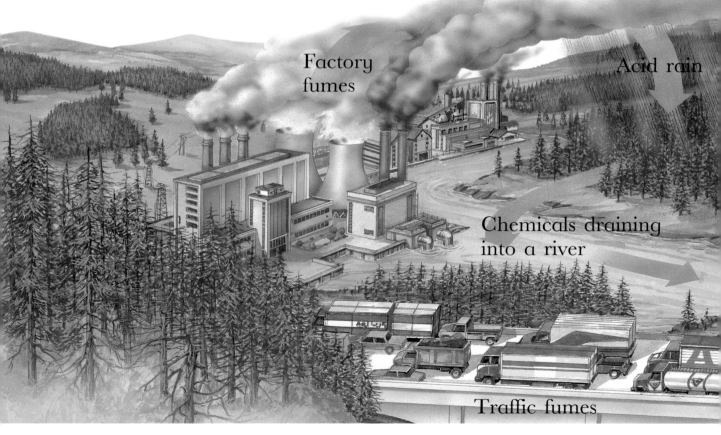

Factory fumes

Acid rain

Chemicals draining into a river

Traffic fumes

Scientists are inventing new forms of energy that don't cause pollution. They can use energy from the sun or wind to make electricity.

Solar-powered electric car

RECYCLE IT!

Sort your family's garbage into boxes for paper, glass, and aluminum cans. Take them to your local recycling center.

Animals are hunted and their homes are destroyed or polluted. The humpback whale (below) has been hunted so much that it may become extinct.

Humpback whale

Prehistoric Life

Evolution

The Earth is millions of years old and is changing slowly all the time. As the Earth changes, so do the plants and animals that live here. They adapt according to where they live. The way that living things change is called evolution.

The first tiny fish lived in the sea about 500 million years ago.

About 395 million years ago, some animals moved onto the land. These were the amphibians.

Most of the animals that live on Earth today didn't exist in the past. Most of the animals that lived in the past no longer exist today. The first plants and animals were tiny and lived in the sea. Nowadays, there are all sorts of living things on every part of the planet.

Some animals become extinct, or die out, if their homes and lives are disturbed. The dodo was a large flightless bird that lived on the island of Mauritius. It was hunted by the people who first moved to the island and is now extinct.

Dinosaurs and other reptiles lived from 240 million years ago to 64 million years ago.

After the dinosaurs died out, mammals took over. The first ones were small, but later ones were larger.

The first humans lived about two million years ago. They may have evolved from apelike creatures.

Dinosaur world

Dinosaurs appeared on our planet 228 million years ago. Some of them were enormous—the biggest animals to ever live on land. Others weren't much bigger than a chicken. They all died out about 64 million years ago.

All dinosaurs had scaly skins and laid eggs, like reptiles today. Some ate plants, while others were hunters. They lived alongside other reptiles and early kinds of birds and insects.

Many dinosaurs
lived near swamps.

1. Stegosaurus
2. Apatosaurus
3. Deinosuchus
4. Allosaurus
5. Archaeopteryx

Plant-eaters

The biggest dinosaurs of all were plant-eaters. They had barrel-shaped bodies and very long necks and tails. They lived in herds and moved around looking for food. They plucked leaves from high in the trees, as giraffes do today.

The weather was warm and wet at the time of the dinosaurs. There were forests of giant ferns and evergreens. Plant-eaters ate leaves, roots, and pinecones. They had peglike teeth for snipping leaves off trees.

1. Brachiosaurus
2. Apatosaurus
3. Diplodocus

Some plant-eaters looked
very strange. One was
called Parasaurolophus.
These dinosaurs had
mouths like beaks
and bony crests
on their heads. They could
blow out through these, and
may have tooted like
trombones.

DINOSAUR INVITE

Draw and color
a long-necked
dinosaur on
a wide piece of
construction paper. Fill in
your party details on the
back. Fold the paper as shown
into an accordion.

Meat-eaters

Some dinosaurs ate animals, and often other dinosaurs. Most meat-eaters were fierce and could move fast to catch their prey. Some of them hunted alone. Others hunted in packs.

Tyrannosaurus Rex was the biggest meat-eater of all. It had massive jaws and razor-sharp teeth for slicing through flesh.

Many meat-eaters had huge hooked claws for slashing out at the animals they chased.

Meat-eating dinosaurs didn't need to eat every day. One kill would provide enough food for several days. Some dinosaurs didn't hunt at all. Instead, they were scavengers, eating any dead or dying animals they found.

Asrovenator

Into battle

Plant-eating dinosaurs couldn't move very fast, so they had to defend themselves against hungry meat-eaters. Some plant-eaters grouped together for safety. Others had fierce horns to scare off enemies, and thick skin like armor.

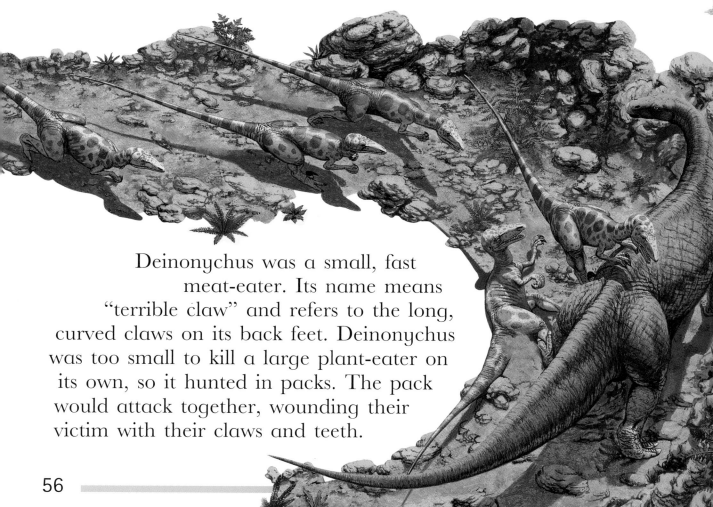

Deinonychus was a small, fast meat-eater. Its name means "terrible claw" and refers to the long, curved claws on its back feet. Deinonychus was too small to kill a large plant-eater on its own, so it hunted in packs. The pack would attack together, wounding their victim with their claws and teeth.

Triceratops was armed with horns on its nose and above its eyes. It also had a huge bony neck shield and thick, leathery skin to help protect itself from enemies.

This armored dinosaur was called Euoplocephalus. It had bony plates and spikes along its back and a huge club at the end of its tail.

A TRICERATOPS MASK

Draw a Triceratops face like this on construction paper. Make a nose horn out of paper and attach it to the mask with a paper fastener. Tie a piece of thin elastic through holes at the sides of the mask.

Hatching out

Dinosaur babies hatched from eggs, just like reptiles do today. Some dinosaur mothers, including Maiasaura, made big nests on the ground in which they laid about 20 eggs. In 1984, a group of more than 20 Maiasaura nests was found on Egg Mountain in Montana.

Dinosaur eggs

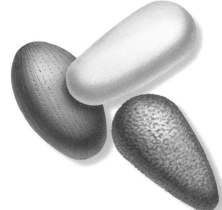

Fossils of dinosaur eggs are different shapes and sizes.

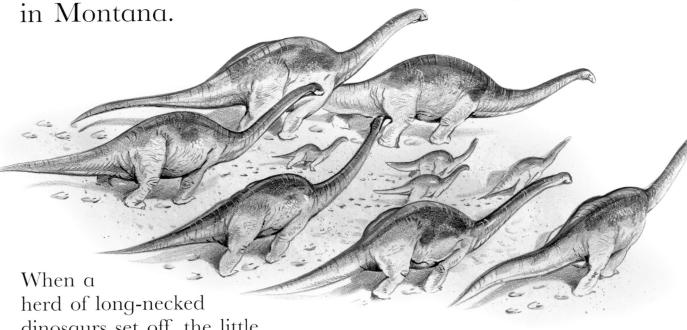

When a herd of long-necked dinosaurs set off, the little ones walked in the middle, protected by the enormous grown-ups.

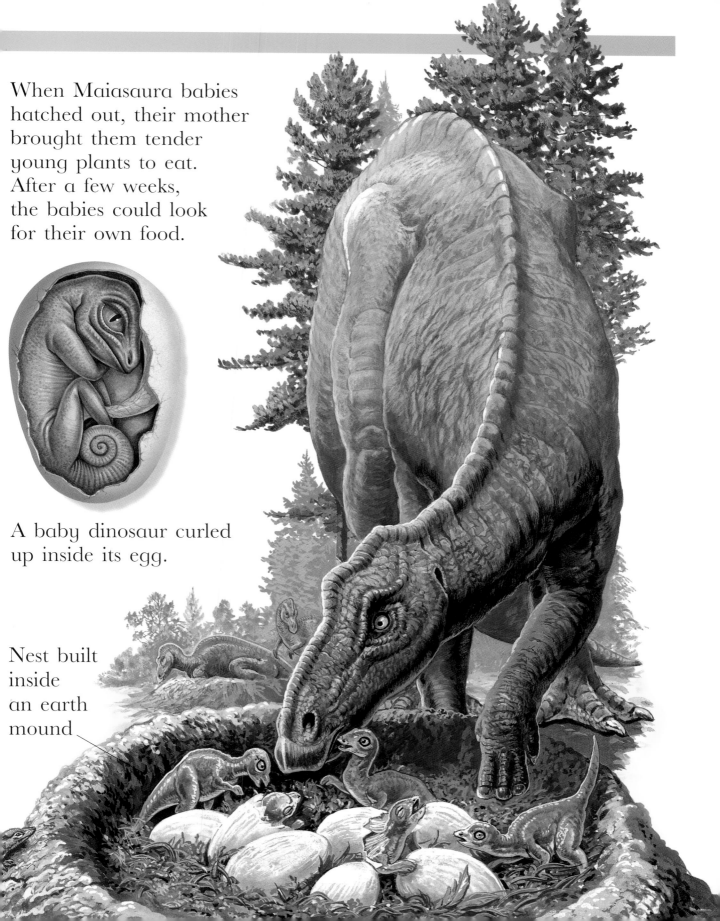

When Maiasaura babies hatched out, their mother brought them tender young plants to eat. After a few weeks, the babies could look for their own food.

A baby dinosaur curled up inside its egg.

Nest built inside an earth mound

Giants of the sea

While dinosaurs ruled the land, many fierce reptiles lived in the sea. Some of them were fast swimmers and looked like dolphins. Others were like lizards, or had strange long necks and giant flippers like paddles.

Kronosaurus had a huge head—bigger than a car.

Mosasaurus was a fierce sea lizard. It crushed small sea creatures in its powerful jaws.

Elasmosaurus had a long snakelike neck. It may have swum along holding its neck and tiny head above the water.

Ichthyosaurus looked like one of today's dolphins. It was a fast swimmer and may have hunted in shoals. It ate fish and creatures like squid.

Teleosaurus was a sea crocodile. It could quickly snap up fish in its long snout armed with sharp teeth.

Take to the skies

The first creatures to fly
were insects, 300 million years ago.
Later, reptiles called pterosaurs took to
the air. They glided across the sky, soaring
above the dinosaurs on the ground.

Archaeopteryx was the first
creature with feathers. It was
half dinosaur and half bird.
No one knows if
it could fly.

Quetzalcoatlus was a giant pterosaur, much, much bigger than even the largest birds today. Its huge wings were made of skin, like a bat's wings. It had a furry body and no feathers or teeth.

The first insects with wings were dragonflies. Meganeura was a huge dragonfly with a wingspan of about 30 inches.

FLY A PTEROSAUR

Take two dowels, one twice as long as the other, and tie together as shown. Get an adult to cut notches in the ends. Make a frame by tying string to each corner. Lay the frame on a clear plastic bag, and cut two inches around the it. Stretch the bag on the frame and tape the edges down. Cut out a pterosaur and tape it to the kite. Tie some string on it to fly the kite.

Extinction

Dinosaurs lived on Earth for 165 million years before they became extinct, dying out forever. All the flying reptiles, sea reptiles, and many other animals died out at the same time. No one knows exactly why.

There are many ideas about why dinosaurs disappeared. Some people think that mammals might have stolen and eaten too many dinosaur eggs. Others think that the weather and living conditions changed, and that it may have become too hot or too cold for dinosaurs.

Some scientists think that a giant meteorite crashed into the Earth about 65 million years ago. Dust from the crash may have blocked out the Sun, so that it was cold and no plants could grow. Plant-eating animals would have starved to death. Meat-eaters would have soon died out too, when there were no other dinosaurs for them to eat.

First people

For most of Earth's history, there have been no humans. The first people like us lived only about 100,000 years ago. They may have been related to apelike creatures that lived earlier.

People living 15,000 years ago survived by hunting, fishing, and gathering plants to eat. They moved from place to place in search of food, and took shelter in caves and tents.

Making a fire

Some people lived in caves in France. They painted pictures of the animals they hunted on their cave walls, using colors made from crushed rocks.

People hunted woolly mammoths. They were huge, and had long, thick hair to protect them from the icy cold weather.

Draw a big woolly mammoth on a large piece of construction paper, copying the picture on the right. Color in its tusks, toes, and eyes. To make its hairy coat, cut short pieces of reddish-brown yarn and glue them to the picture. If you want to, you can cut it out.

Making tools

Early people were good at making things with their hands. Remains found in their caves show that they made knives and weapons from sharp stones, and tools from antlers, bones, and mammoth tusks.

67

Plant Life

Plants everywhere

There are millions of different kinds of plants. They grow nearly everywhere in the world. They can be all shapes and sizes, from tiny mosses to enormous trees. Some spring up after it rains in hot, dry deserts. Others flower in snowy cracks high on mountains.

In steamy rain forests, many plants grow high above the ground on sunny tree branches. These plants are called epiphytes. They soak up all the water they need from the damp air or collect rainwater in their cup-shaped leaves.

Like many plants, the rose has beautiful flowers. Roses often smell sweet.

Oak
tree

Acorn

Trees are the largest plants in the world. Some, such as the oak, can live to be hundreds of years old. The oak produces seeds called acorns.

Fungi are not plants. They do not have leaves or roots, and they are not green. Instead of seeds, they produce spores.

Some plants live underwater. Thick forests of rubbery seaweed grow in sand and mud at the bottom of the sea.

Food for growth

Plants need food and water to grow. Their roots take water from the soil and their leaves take in air and sunlight. Plants use water, air, and sunlight to make their own food.

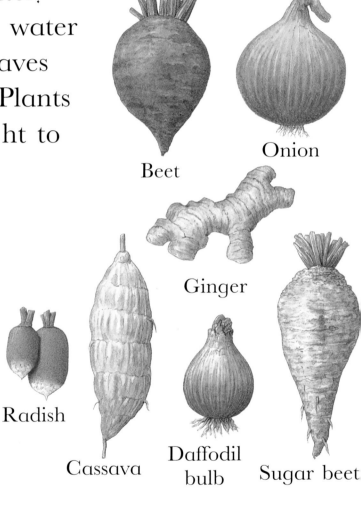

Beet

Onion

Ginger

Radish

Cassava

Daffodil bulb

Sugar beet

TAKE A CUTTING

Spider plants grow baby plants at the ends of long stems. Snip off a baby plant and put it in a glass of water. When it has grown roots, plant it in a small pot of moist soil.

All plants have roots. Some plants have fat roots, others have swollen buds or stems under the ground. These are used to store food. Plants use the food stored in them to grow when conditions are right.

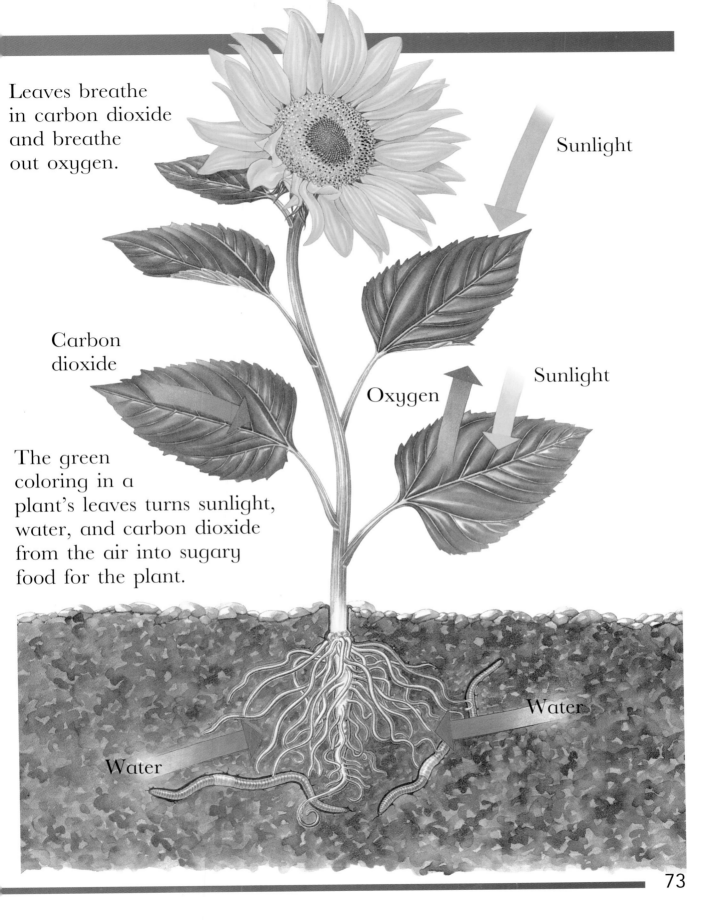

Leaves breathe in carbon dioxide and breathe out oxygen.

Sunlight

Carbon dioxide

Oxygen

Sunlight

The green coloring in a plant's leaves turns sunlight, water, and carbon dioxide from the air into sugary food for the plant.

Water

Water

Flowers

Flowers come in nearly every color, and many different shapes—bells, circles, stars, and trumpets. Garden flowers are often the showy relatives of simple wildflowers.

A meadow is full of flowers in the spring and summer. Butterflies and other insects visit the flowers because they like their color and scent.

Poppies

Buttercups

Some flowers, like this orchid, are rare and only grow in a few places. It is important not to pick rare plants so that they can make seeds for new plants.

Daisies

PRESS FLOWERS

Lay fresh flowers between pieces of newspaper in a book. Shut the book and put something heavy on top. Leave for four weeks, then use the flowers to decorate cards and bookmarks.

Clover

Making seeds

To make seeds, a flower needs pollen from another flower. Most flowers contain a sweet juice called nectar that birds and insects drink. As they drink, they brush against pollen, which they carry from flower to flower. This is called pollination.

Tiny hummingbirds pollinate some flowers in hot countries. They push their beaks right into the flowers to reach the nectar inside.

Pollen

Hibiscus flowers attract hummingbirds.

Many flowers are pollinated by insects. The bee orchid tricks bees into thinking it is a female bee. Bees land on it and pick up the flower's sticky pollen.

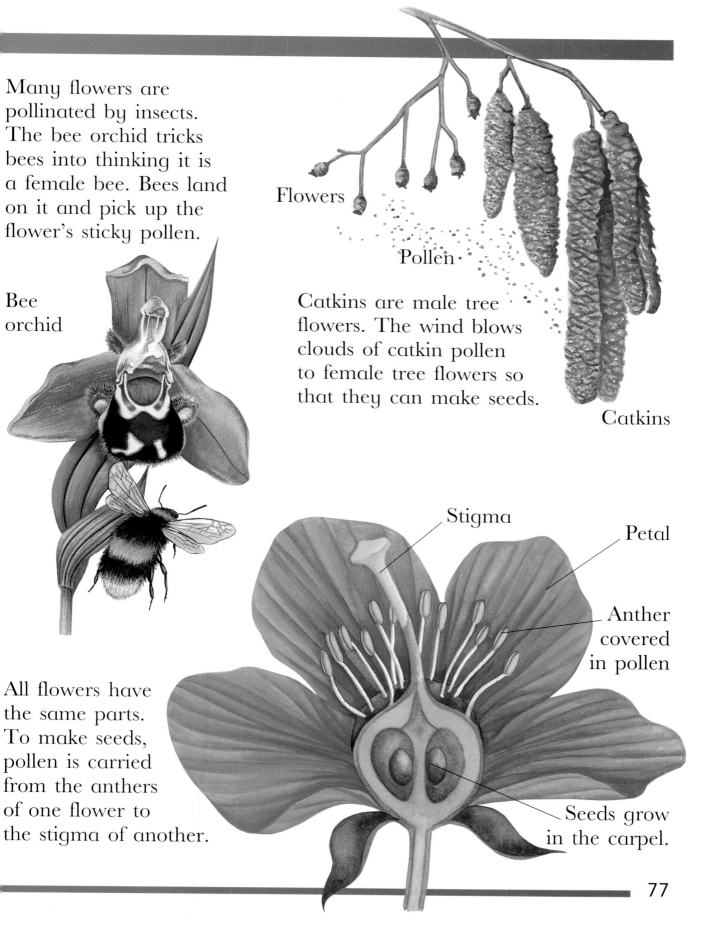

Flowers

Pollen

Catkins are male tree flowers. The wind blows clouds of catkin pollen to female tree flowers so that they can make seeds.

Catkins

Bee orchid

Stigma

Petal

Anther covered in pollen

All flowers have the same parts. To make seeds, pollen is carried from the anthers of one flower to the stigma of another.

Seeds grow in the carpel.

Fruits and berries

After a flower has been pollinated, seeds start to grow. They are protected by a soft fruit which grows around the seeds. Some fruits only contain one big seed or stone. Berries have a lot of tiny seeds inside them.

Look for these berries in the picture:

1. Hawthorn berries
2. Rosehips
3. Blackberries
4. Elderberries
5. Rowan berries

In the fall, hedges are full of ripe, juicy berries. These are eaten by birds and animals. Later, the seeds inside the berries are scattered on the ground in bird and animal droppings.

Ask an adult to slice the top off a pumpkin. Scoop out the seeds and flesh. Cut holes in the pumpkin to make it look like a face. Wedge a short candle in the base of the pumpkin and ask an adult to light it for you.

4

5

All trees make fruits. These contain seeds that can grow into new trees. Some fruits, such as oranges, are soft. Nuts are tree fruits with hard shells around them.

Orange tree

79

Seeds

Most plants grow from seeds which fall on the ground. In the spring, the soil is damp and warm. This makes each seed swell and start to grow. The root grows first, then a shoot. This is called germination.

Seeds inside berries often reach the ground in bird droppings.

Dandelion seeds are blown to the ground by the wind.

Bean seed

Root Shoot

When a seed germinates, it splits open and a root begins to grow. A leafy shoot pushes up through the soil toward the light. Leaves help the plant to make its own food.

First real leaves

Stem

MINIGARDEN

Wad some tissues into two clean eggshells. Sprinkle alfalfa seeds on top and keep the tissues damp. In ten days you will be able to cut some sprouts.

Some seeds are hidden inside soft, juicy fruit. Others have hard shells to protect them— these are called nuts.

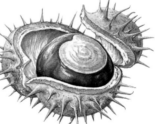

Horse chestnut

Peach

Pine cone

Sycamore

Plants and animals

Without plants, there would not be any animals. Plants provide all kinds of animals with food and homes. In return, animals help to scatter the seeds that will grow into new plants.

Harvest mouse

Harvest mice eat grass seeds, like a lot of other small animals. The spiky seedheads of some plants stick to their fur and are carried to different places, where the seeds fall off and grow.

Some animals eat only one kind of food. Koalas live in eucalyptus trees in Australia. They eat nothing but the juicy eucalyptus leaves.

Goldfinches also feed on seeds. They crush them in their beaks. Some of the seeds are scattered on the ground in bird droppings.

Leaf-cutter ants snip up leaves and carry them to their nest, where they chew them into a pulp. The ants feed on fungus that grows on the leaves.

Plants we eat

Many of the things we eat and drink are made from plants. Fruits and vegetables come from plants, and so do flour, sugar, coffee, and chocolate. Nearly all plant foods are grown as crops by farmers around the world.

The vegetables we eat come from different parts of vegetable plants. Some are roots, such as carrots. Others may come from the leaves, stems, pods, or seeds of plants.

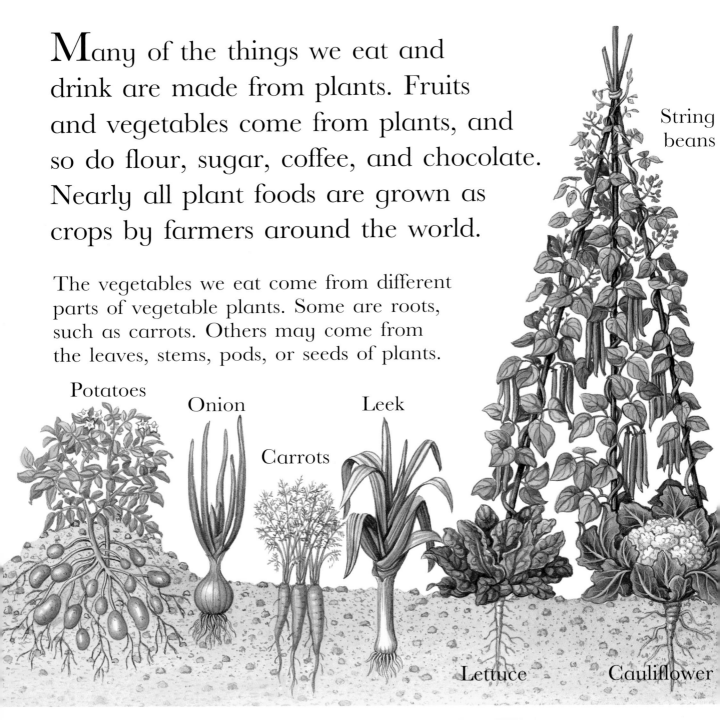

String beans

Potatoes

Onion

Carrots

Leek

Lettuce

Cauliflower

Grapes

Olives

Fruit grows on bushes, trees, and vines. Grapes are often made into wine, and olives can be pressed to make olive oil.

Cereals are grasses grown for their seeds or grain, such as wheat, oats, and rice. Many are ground into flour or made into breakfast cereals.

LETTUCE IN A POT

Fill a shallow tray with soil. Sprinkle lettuce seeds on top. Spray the seeds with water and cover with a clear plastic bag. Keep the soil moist and remove the bag when tiny plants appear. Plant them in their own pots when they grow bigger.

Animal World

What is a reptile?

Snakes, lizards, crocodiles, and turtles are all reptiles. They have dry, scaly skin. Reptiles are cold-blooded. This means that their bodies are the same temperature as their surroundings. They lie in the sun to warm up, then hide in the shade to cool down.

Most reptiles hatch from eggs, like this baby snake. Reptile eggs do not have hard shells. Instead, they are soft and leathery.

Gecko

Snakes and lizards, such as this gecko, shed their skins as they grow. A new layer of skin is ready underneath.

A snake does not smell things with its nose, but with its forked tongue. It flickers its tongue in and out to track down food.

Forked tongue

The frilled lizard spreads out its neck frill to make itself look very fierce and frighten away enemies.

Frilled lizard

Lizards

Geckos, iguanas, skinks, and chameleons are all lizards. They usually live on the ground, but some spend their lives scuttling in the treetops or burrowing underground. Most lizards eat insects.

Many lizards are brightly colored and patterned. This eyed lizard gets its name from the blue spots along its sides.

The Gila monster is a poisonous lizard. It makes poison in its mouth and bites small animals to kill them.

The horned lizard looks scary, but it is actually harmless.

A chameleon is a type of tree lizard whose tongue is as long as its body. It shoots its tongue out very fast to catch insects.

The Komodo dragon (below) is the largest lizard in the world, and is very fierce. It has sharp, jagged teeth, a bit like a shark's.

Chameleon

Komodo dragon

The chameleon changes color to match the things around it. This makes it hard to spot in the treetops.

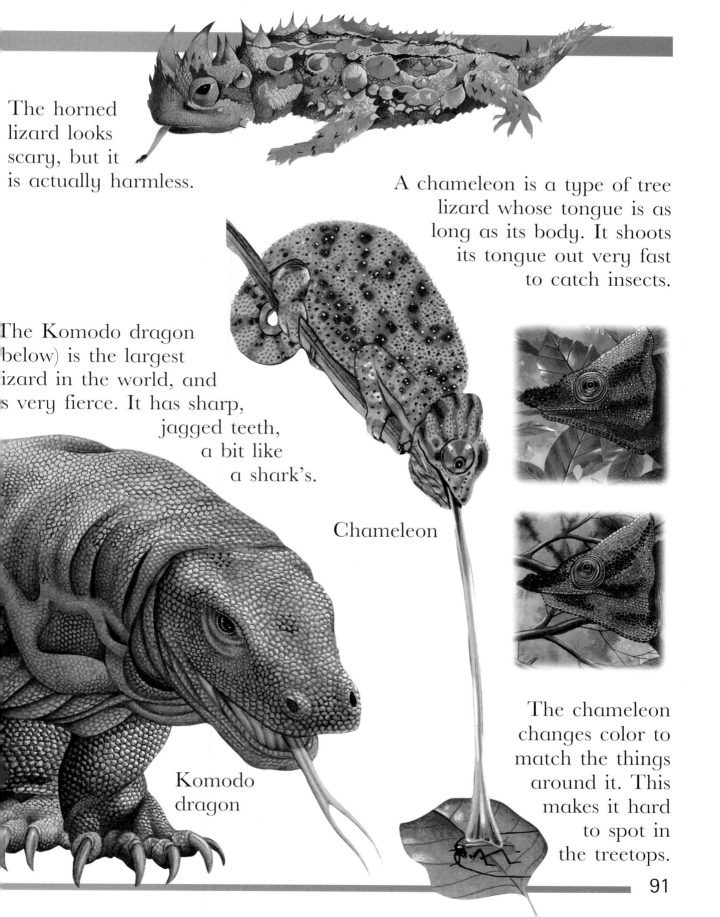

Turtles

Turtles and tortoises are the only reptiles with a heavy shell to protect them from enemies. Some turtles live on land, and some in the sea or in fresh water. Tortoises live only on land. Turtles and tortoises both lay their eggs on land.

2. The turtle digs a hole. She lays her eggs in it and covers them with sand.

1. A turtle swims to a sandy beach at night to lay her eggs.

3. When the baby turtles hatch, they climb out of the sand and run to the sea.

A tortoise moves very slowly. When something scares it, it tucks its head and legs right inside its shell.

MAKE A TURTLE

Make a hole in each side of a styrofoam bowl. Thread some elastic through the holes and tie the ends. Glue brown paper patches around the bottom of the bowl. Glue paper eyes to the middle finger of a glove. Put on the glove and wear the bowl on top.

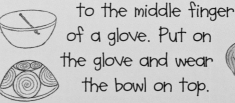

Giant tortoises live on the Galapagos Islands. They may live for up to 50 years and grow to be three feet long.

Crocodiles

Crocodiles usually live in rivers in hot countries. They spend most of their time lying in the water, waiting for animals to come to drink. Then they lunge forward to attack. Few animals can escape their sharp teeth.

Crocodiles float with their eyes and nose above the surface.

Alligator

Garial

Caiman

The three animals above are all related to the crocodile. Each one has a different snout.

An alligator (above) lies on a sunny riverbank to warm up. It cools down by rolling around in deep pools of water.

A mother crocodile (below) looks after her eggs. When they hatch, she carries the babies gently down to the river in her huge mouth.

Frogs

Frogs live in many different places. Some can even be found high up in the treetops. All frogs lay their eggs in water. The tiny creatures that hatch do not look like frogs at first, but they change as they grow. This is called metamorphosis.

A frog can leap a long way because its back legs are like springs. It starts with them folded. To jump, it unfolds its long back legs and springs forward.

1. A frog lays hundreds of eggs. The eggs are laid in a clear jelly. These are known as frogspawn.

Mother frog

2. Tadpoles grow inside the eggs.

Tree frogs have sticky pads on their fingers and toes to help them grip tree branches.

FROG LEAPS

See if you can jump like a frog. Squat down and put your hands on the floor between your feet. Take a giant leap forward and land in the same position. Why not have a frog race with your friends?

3. The eggs hatch into tadpoles.

4. The tadpoles grow bigger and develop legs.

5. The tadpoles turn into frogs and leave the water.

What is a fish?

Fish live in water and are amazing swimmers. Some fish are as small as tadpoles and others longer than crocodiles. Some are flat and others tube-shaped. But most fish have the same basic features.

Slippery scales on a fish's body help it to glide smoothly through the water.

Most fish lay eggs. They lay hundreds of tiny eggs at a time.

Fish use their fins to steer and turn as they swim.

A fish does not have eyelids, so it always swims with its eyes wide open.

Some fish live in the sea, where the water is salty. Others live in rivers and lakes. These are called freshwater fish.

Fish have slits called gills on the sides of their heads so that they can breathe under water.

A fish swims along by beating its tail from side to side.

AN AQUARIUM

Paint the inside of a shoebox blue-green. Turn the box onto its side and put pebbles and shells inside it. Draw, color, and cut out some pretty fish. Tape a string to each fish and tape them to the top of the box.

Coral fish

Thousands of brightly colored fish dart through the clear blue waters around a coral reef. Corals grow in many shapes and colors, like a rocky garden under the sea. The water is shallow and sunny, and there is plenty to eat.

1

3

2

Most of the fish that live on coral reefs have colorful spots or stripes. This makes it hard for a hunter to spot them swimming through the corals.

1. Trumpet fish
2. Cowfish
3. Parrot fish
4. Butterfly fish
5. Lion fish
6. Angel fish

Sea hunters

Many of the creatures that live in the sea feed on plants, but others are fierce and deadly hunters. Some sea hunters rely on speed to catch their prey, but others have more unusual ways of finding their food.

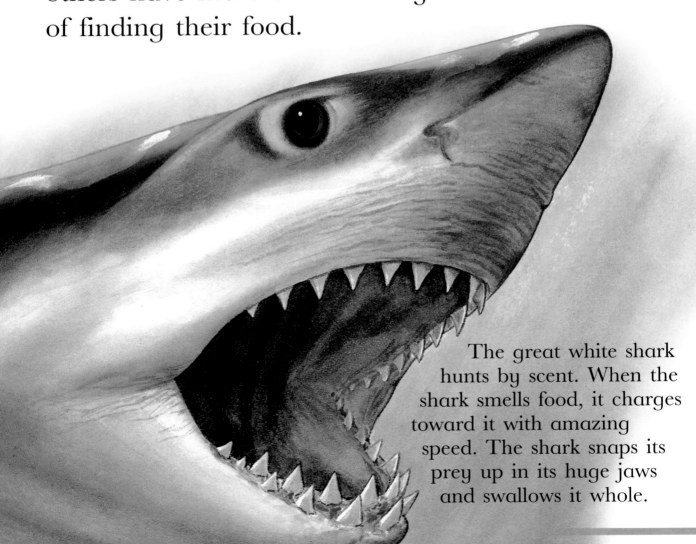

The great white shark hunts by scent. When the shark smells food, it charges toward it with amazing speed. The shark snaps its prey up in its huge jaws and swallows it whole.

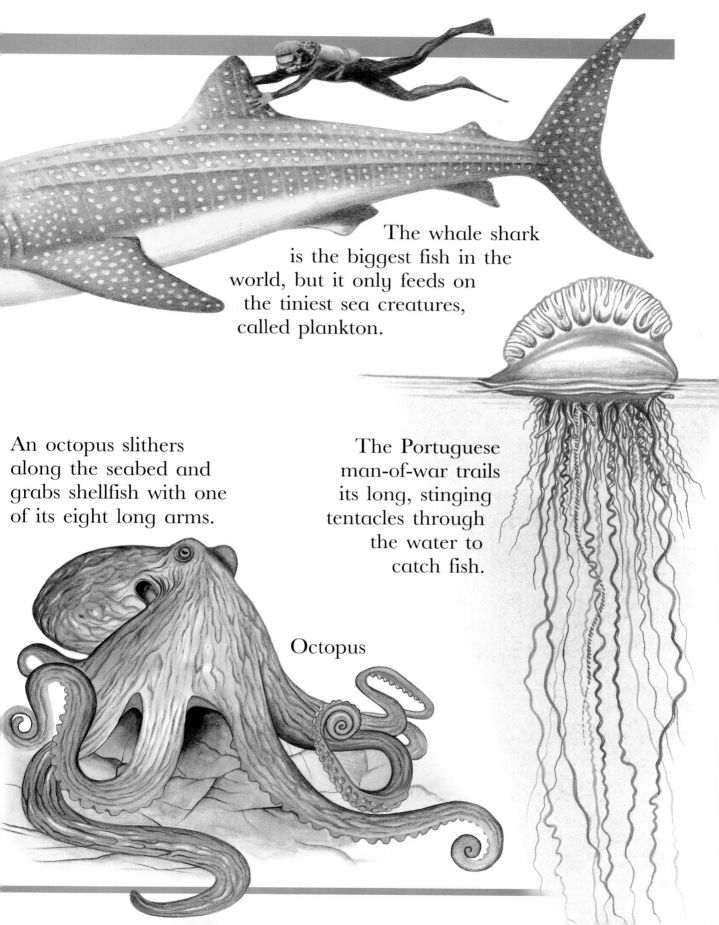

The whale shark is the biggest fish in the world, but it only feeds on the tiniest sea creatures, called plankton.

An octopus slithers along the seabed and grabs shellfish with one of its eight long arms.

The Portuguese man-of-war trails its long, stinging tentacles through the water to catch fish.

Octopus

What is an insect?

Most insects are small. Their bodies are made up of three parts—a head, a thorax (middle), and an abdomen (back part). An insect has six legs and two antennae. Its body is protected by a hard outer case.

Thorax

Head

Proboscis

Honeybees feed on nectar, a sweet juice inside flowers. They suck up the nectar through a feeding tube called a proboscis. Honeybees also collect flower pollen.

Antennae

The wings of the brightly colored shield bug are hidden beneath the large striped shield on its back.

Ants live in colonies.

Wing

Abdomen

A butterfly has four wings. It folds them above its back when resting.

This leaf insect looks just like the leaf it is sitting on. It is very hard for hungry animals to see it.

Tiny clawed leg

A stick insect looks like a twig.

Termites live in huge groups called colonies. Their giant nests, made of mud and sand, protect the queen termite in the middle.

Termite

Butterflies

On a warm summer day, butterflies flutter from flower to flower, feeding on nectar. The beautiful patterns on a butterfly's wings are made of thousands of brightly colored, overlapping scales. Moths are like butterflies, but fly at night.

Monarch butterfly

A butterfly begins life as a wriggly caterpillar. It has to change completely before it becomes a butterfly.

1. A butterfly lays its eggs on a plant.

2. The eggs hatch into caterpillars.

3. The caterpillars eat and grow bigger.

Tiger moth

Moths have fatter bodies than butterflies and their antennae are not as thick as butterfly antennae. Moth antennae are feathery or look like hairs.

The death's-head moth has a shape like a skull on the back of its head.

Cinnabar moth

4. Each caterpillar turns into a pupa.

5. A butterfly breaks out of the pupa.

Minimonsters

There are many tiny creatures that are not insects and cannot fly. Most of them hide away among plants or stones during the day. They usually come out to look for food at night, or just after it has rained.

An earthworm eats the soil as it wriggles its way through. It has no eyes, ears, or legs.

Stinger

Scorpions usually live in hot countries. They are very fierce. A scorpion catches its prey in its giant pincers and kills it with the poisonous stinger at the end of its tail.

Pincer

The hairy tarantula is one of the biggest spiders in the world.

HAIRY SPIDER

Make a pompom by winding yarn around two cardboard disks with holes in the middle. Push four pipe cleaners through the holes. Cut around the edge of the cardboard and tie some yarn around the middle. Take out the cardboard. Bend the pipe cleaners to make legs, and stick on eyes.

A centipede has a lot of tiny legs. There is one pair of legs on each segment of its body.

Snails slither along the ground, leaving trails of slime behind them. If they are scared, they quickly draw back into their shells.

What is a bird?

There are thousands of different birds of every color, shape, and size. Birds are the only animals that have feathers, and most birds can fly. The smallest bird is no bigger than a butterfly. The largest is taller than a man.

The tiny wren is only about as long as your finger.

A bird's body is a clever flying machine. Birds have very light bones and strong wing muscles to make it easier to fly. Their feathers keep them warm and dry. A bird's tail helps it to steer and brake when it is flying.

The shape of a bird's beak shows what kind of food it eats. The toucan's giant bill is good for plucking fruit.

The ostrich cannot fly. It is the biggest and heaviest bird of all.

The peregrine's smooth shape helps it to fly and dive very fast.

Birds of prey

Birds of prey are fierce hunters with sharp beaks and claws, and very good eyesight. They soar high in the sky, hunting for small animals or fish. When they spot an animal moving beneath them, they swoop down from the sky and kill it.

Eagles are the biggest birds of prey. They have long, sharp claws called talons, and they attack feetfirst. The bald eagle catches fish. It swoops down to the water, grabs a fish and carries it away.

Owls hunt at night and can see well even in the dark. Fringed feathers at the edges of their wings help them fly without a sound.

Groups of vultures gather at a kill. Vultures are scavengers. They usually eat animals that are already dead.

BEAKY BIRD CARD

Fold some construction paper in half and cut a slit in the middle. Fold back the corners and push them inside out. Glue the card to more

paper, leaving the beak free. Draw a bird's face around the beak. Now open and close the card.

Water birds

Many birds live near water. Some of them are good at swimming and some just wade at the water's edge. Seabirds feed on fish from the sea. Other birds nest close to rivers or lakes, where there is also plenty of food.

Ducks, geese, swans, and most seabirds have webbed feet. These help them swim quickly.

Puffins dive into the sea to catch fish. Their colorful beaks are so big that they can hold several small fish at a time. Huge groups of puffins make their nests on steep cliffs.

The heron has long legs like stilts and a sharp beak like a dagger. It stands very still at the edge of a river or lake, waiting for fish. When the heron spots one, it stabs it with its beak and gulps it down.

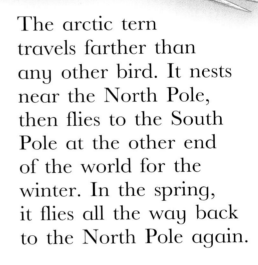

The arctic tern travels farther than any other bird. It nests near the North Pole, then flies to the South Pole at the other end of the world for the winter. In the spring, it flies all the way back to the North Pole again.

Penguins fish in the icy cold seas near the South Pole. They have short wings like flippers and swim so fast that they look as if they are flying through the water.

Nests and eggs

All birds lay eggs that hatch into chicks. Most birds make soft nests in which to lay their eggs. They build them in safe places, away from enemies. Then the birds sit on their eggs to keep them warm until they hatch.

When a chick is ready to hatch, it uses a special tooth to chip a hole in its shell. When the hole is big enough, the chick pushes its way out, headfirst.

Crows build big, messy nests high in treetops. The nests are made of sticks bound together with mud and moss. Inside, they are lined with a thick layer of soft wool or hair.

The chicks squawk for food.

The Indian tailor bird makes its nest by sewing leaves together with silk from a spider's web.

Swallows build cup-shaped mud nests high up on walls, out of reach of enemies.

The chicks are covered in fluffy down.

The plover does not make a nest. Instead, it lays its eggs on gravel, where the speckled eggs are well camouflaged.

Mammals

Mammals are animals whose bodies are covered with fur or hair. They feed their babies on milk. There are many different mammals. Most of them live on land, but some of them live in the sea.

Like many mammals, pigs give birth to several babies at a time. The piglets push and shove to take turns drinking their mother's milk.

White-sided dolphin

Dolphins and whales are mammals that live in the sea. They cannot breathe under water, so they come up to the surface to breathe.

Bats are the only mammals that can fly. They come out to hunt for food at night and roost during the day. Bats have furry bodies and leathery wings that stretch along their arm and finger bones.

A rabbit has a thick furry coat, like many mammals. Its fur keeps it warm and dry and protects it from injury. A rabbit can see, hear, and smell very well. These sharp senses help it to look out for enemies.

119

Hunting

Many mammals are meat-eaters. This means that they have to catch other animals to eat. Animal hunters are armed with sharp teeth and claws, and can usually run very fast. Some animals hunt alone. Others work together to track down their prey.

Wolves and other wild dogs hunt in groups called packs. Each pack has a strong dog as a leader. Wolves work as a team to catch large animals.

The cheetah can run faster than any other animal. It silently slinks as close as it can to its prey, then sprints forwards and takes it by surprise.

Bears kill other animals with a swipe of their massive paws. The brown bear likes fish. It hooks salmon out of the water as they swim upstream to lay their eggs.

Living in a herd

Animals that eat plants spend most of their time grazing on grass or munching leaves. Many of them live on grasslands where there is nowhere to hide from hunters. It is safer for them to live together in large herds.

Wild horses move from place to place in herds. Each herd is made up of female horses and their foals. They are led by a stallion, a male horse.

Mother elephants and their babies live together in family groups, led by an older female. All the adults help take care of the babies.

Wildebeest live in enormous herds. Each herd travels great distances, looking for fresh grass to eat.

MAKE AN ELEPHANT CHAIN

Fold a long piece of paper into wide pleats. Draw an elephant on the top fold, with its trunk and tail touching each side, as shown. Cut out the elephant and unfold the paper to make an elephant chain.

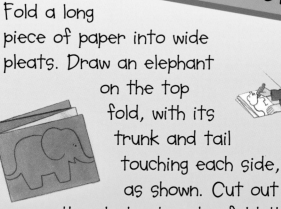

Marsupials

Marsupials are mammals with a pouch that their babies grow in. The babies are very small when they are born. They crawl up into their mother's pouch and live there until they are bigger.

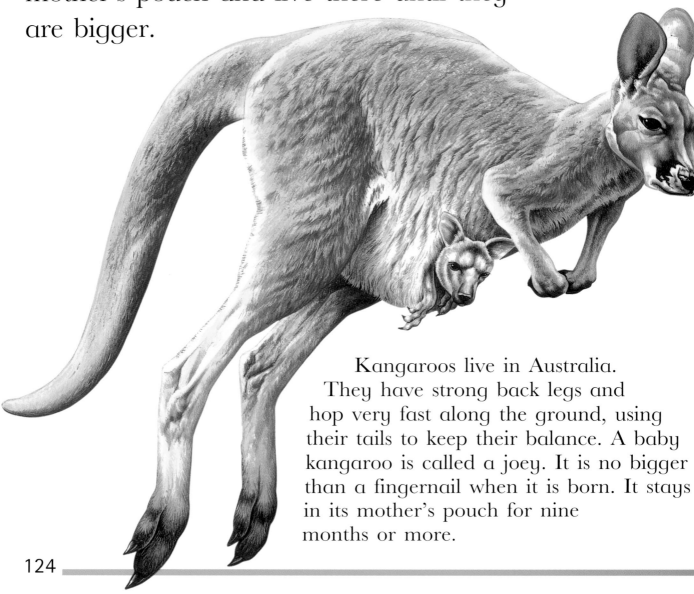

Kangaroos live in Australia. They have strong back legs and hop very fast along the ground, using their tails to keep their balance. A baby kangaroo is called a joey. It is no bigger than a fingernail when it is born. It stays in its mother's pouch for nine months or more.

Koalas are not bears. They are related to opossums. Koalas live in eucalyptus trees in Australia. Eucalyptus leaves are the only thing they eat. The leaves are so juicy that koalas never need to drink.

The Australian possum lives in trees. Baby possums live for 10 weeks in their mother's pouch, then they climb out and cling tightly to her fur.

ROO PENCIL POUCH

Draw a big kangaroo outline on felt and cut it out. Cut out two ears and a pouch. Glue the ears to the kangaroo and sew on the pouch. Draw a face and arms. Glue on beads for eyes.

Water mammals

Some mammals spend most of their time in water. All water mammals are very good swimmers. Many of them dive deep underwater to catch fish. They can stay there for a long time, but they have to return to the surface to breathe.

Otters live by rivers and seas. They have thick waterproof fur to keep them warm when they swim in cold water.

Hippotamuses live in Africa. During the day they stay in rivers and lakes to keep cool. At night they go ashore to find grass and plants to eat.

The blue whale is the biggest animal in the world. It eats tiny shrimp called krill. It sieves them out of the water through a bony fringe in its mouth called a baleen.

Seals live in cold seas. They have a thick layer of fat called blubber to keep them warm. Seals have flippers instead of back legs. They are fast swimmers and chase after fish, squid, and octopus.

Strange mammals

From the tiniest mouse to the biggest whale, mammals come in every shape and size, and some of them are pretty strange.

The armadillo curls up when it is in danger. Its body is protected by bony plates of armor.

The aardvark lives on African grasslands. It eats insects called termites. When it finds a termite mound, it rips it open with its sharp claws and licks up the insects with its long, sticky tongue.

The giraffe has long legs and a very long neck. It can stretch right up into the trees, to pull off juicy leaves and shoots that other animals cannot reach.

The platypus is furry. But it also has a flat beak and webbed feet, like a duck. It is one of the only mammals that lay eggs.

INVENT AN ANIMAL

Fold a long piece of paper into sections, as shown below. With a friend, take turns to draw part of a different animal on each section. When you open the paper out, you will see the animal you have invented!

Animals in danger

Sadly, some animals are in danger of dying out forever. Thousands of animals die every year because their homes are destroyed when forests are chopped down. Other animals are killed by hunters.

Great auks are extinct now. "Extinct" means that an animal has died out. Great auks were hunted for food until there were none left.

Tigers were in danger of dying out in India a few years ago, so a campaign was launched to save them. Special wildlife parks were set up where tigers can live safely.

The giant panda is one of the rarest animals in the world. There are fewer than 1,600 of them left. Pandas live in lonely parts of China. They only eat bamboo. Every few years the bamboo dies off. Some pandas die because they cannot find enough food.

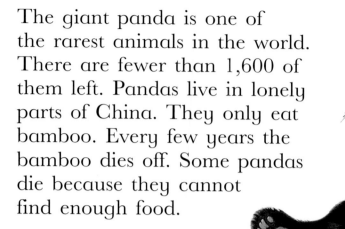

The black rhinoceros lives in Africa and feeds on leaves and twigs. For a long time hunters have killed rhinos for their horns, which are used to make Asian medicines. Now it is against the law to hunt rhinos.

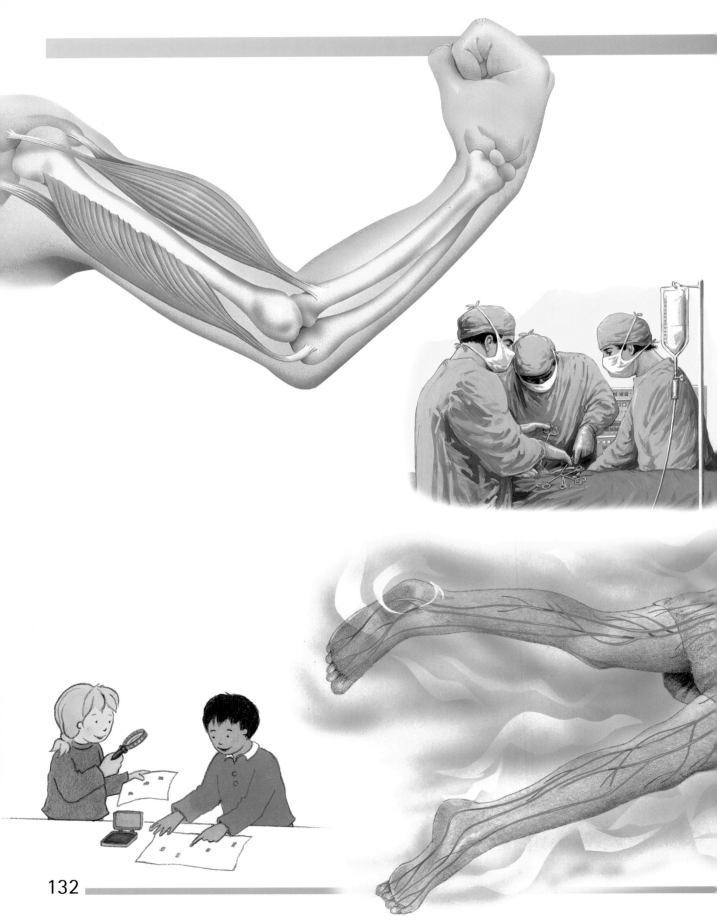

Your Body

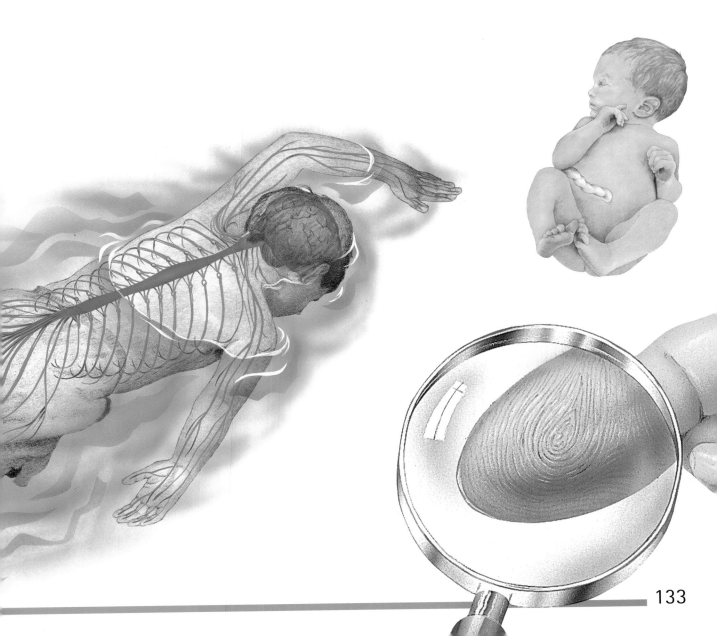

Inside you

Inside your body there are parts called organs that are hard at work all the time. Each organ does a special job that keeps your body working correctly. They all work together like the different parts of a machine.

Your brain, lungs, heart, liver, stomach, and intestines are organs. They receive all the things they need from your blood, as it flows around your body.

Brain

Lungs

Heart

Liver

Stomach

Intestines

Your heart pumps your blood around every part of your body. It beats about 70 times a minute all the time you are alive.

Lay two fingers gently on the inside of your other wrist, below the creases. Count how many beats you feel in 15 seconds. Multiply this by four to find out how often your heart beats in a minute.

Your heart is about the same size as your clenched fist. As you grow, your heart grows bigger and stronger, too.

135

Bones and joints

There are more than 200 bones that together make up your skeleton. This strong framework supports and protects the soft parts of your body. Without it, you would not be able to stand up or move around.

Bones are different shapes and sizes, depending on the job they do. Your skull forms a strong, bony case around your delicate brain. Your ribcage surrounds your chest to protect the organs inside.

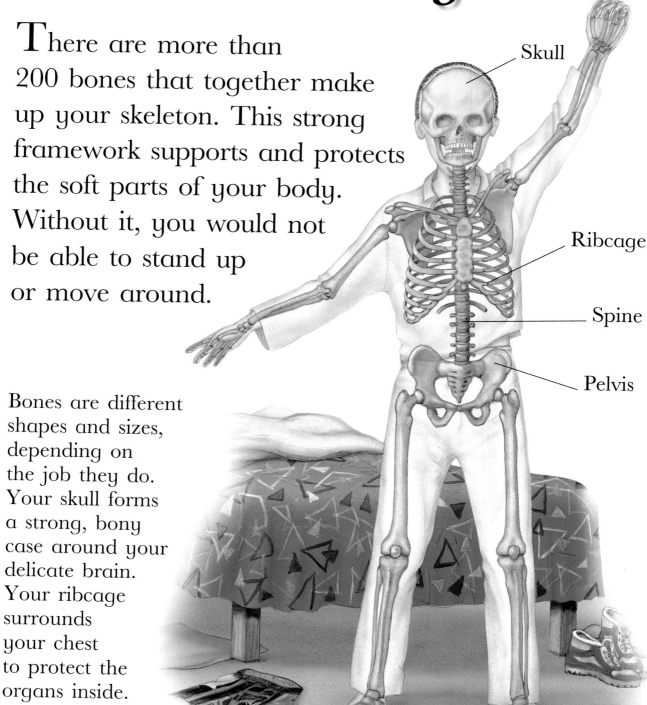

Skull

Ribcage

Spine

Pelvis

136

The place where two bones meet is called a joint. The ends of the bones fit together or slide over each other smoothly.

Basketball

Your joints allow you to perform many different activities.

Soccer

HALLOWEEN SKELETON

Draw a body, arms, and legs like these on black construction paper and cut them out. Make small holes with a pencil point where shown. Attach the arms and legs to the body with paper fasteners. Paint a skeleton on the body, using white paint. Hang the skeleton from a piece of string to scare your friends!

Bicycling

Ballet

Tennis

Baseball

These children are bending and stretching their bodies in all kinds of sports.

Skin and hair

Your body is snugly wrapped up in your skin. Skin is a stretchy, waterproof covering that fits you like a glove. It protects your insides from dirt and germs, and helps to keep your body at the right temperature.

The skin on your fingertips has tiny ridges on it. These help you to grip things. Everyone has a different pattern of ridges.

Skin is not always the same color. A brown coloring called melanin helps protect skin from sunlight. Brown skin contains more melanin than white skin. People from hot, sunny places often have dark skin.

You are always growing new skin, because skin wears away. Hairs grow from the lower layer of your skin. Nerve endings help you feel things. Sweat glands release sweat through tiny holes called pores. This cools you down.

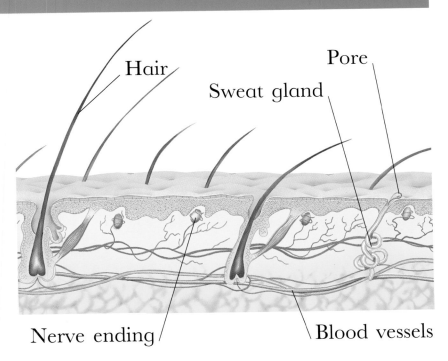

Hair
Sweat gland
Pore
Nerve ending
Blood vessels

When you are cold, you look pale because the blood vessels in your skin narrow to keep you from losing more heat. Your hairs stand on end to trap body heat, and you shiver to warm up.

DETECTIVE WORK

To take a friend's fingerprints, roll each finger lightly on an ink pad, then press it firmly on a piece of paper. Examine the prints with a magnifying glass to see the pattern on them.

The brain

Your brain is the control center of your whole body. It keeps all the different parts working, and it never shuts down. Every time you move, your brain sends a message to part of your body, telling it what to do. You also use your brain to think and feel.

Your nerves are like a system of wires that run from your brain all around your body. They carry millions of messages between your brain and the rest of your body.

Nerves carry messages at very high speed, so that you can react quickly to whatever is happening around you.

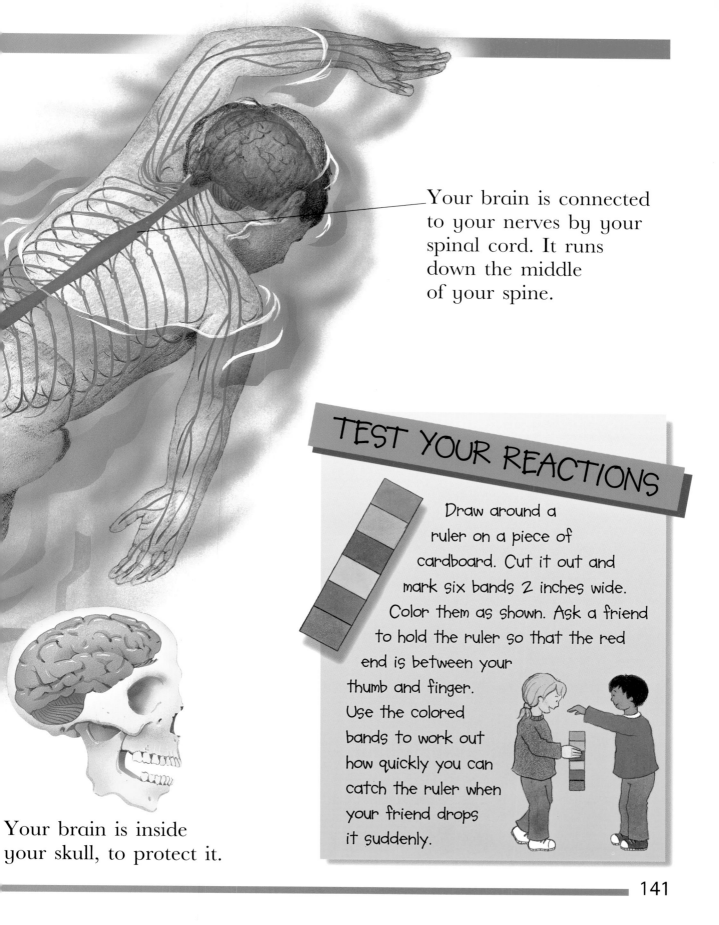

Your brain is connected to your nerves by your spinal cord. It runs down the middle of your spine.

Your brain is inside your skull, to protect it.

TEST YOUR REACTIONS

Draw around a ruler on a piece of cardboard. Cut it out and mark six bands 2 inches wide. Color them as shown. Ask a friend to hold the ruler so that the red end is between your thumb and finger. Use the colored bands to work out how quickly you can catch the ruler when your friend drops it suddenly.

Muscles

You have more than 600 muscles that help you move every part of your body. Every time you jump, chew, or just blink, you use different muscles. The brain controls all the muscles in your body, even when you are asleep.

This muscle tightens to bend your arm

Tendon

This muscle tightens to straighten your arm

Muscles are joined to bones by cords of tissue called tendons. Muscles tighten to move bones. They only pull, so they usually work in pairs.

This gymnast is using hundreds of different muscles. She exercises to make her muscles stronger so she can bend, stretch, and jump more easily.

FUNNY FACE TRICKS

Some of the tiny muscles in your face are very hard to use. Have a competition with your friends to see who can waggle their ears, flare their nostrils, or arch their eyebrows—without moving any other part of their face at the same time.

Muscles in your face are hard at work all the time. Tiny muscles in your eyelids tighten to make you blink and wash your eyes with tears. You do this about 20,000 times a day!

Breathing

You breathe all the time, even when you are asleep. The air that you breathe into your lungs contains a gas called oxygen, which you need to stay alive. Your lungs take oxygen from the air, then your blood carries it all around your body.

Windpipe

Lungs

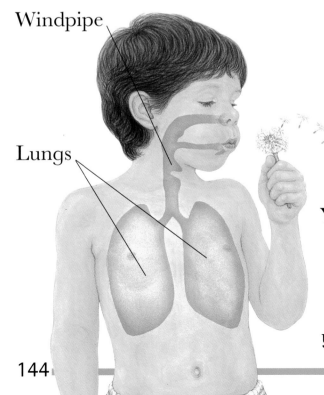

Your lungs are like big sponges. When you breathe in, they fill with air. When you breathe out or blow, they push out a waste gas called carbon dioxide that your body doesn't need.

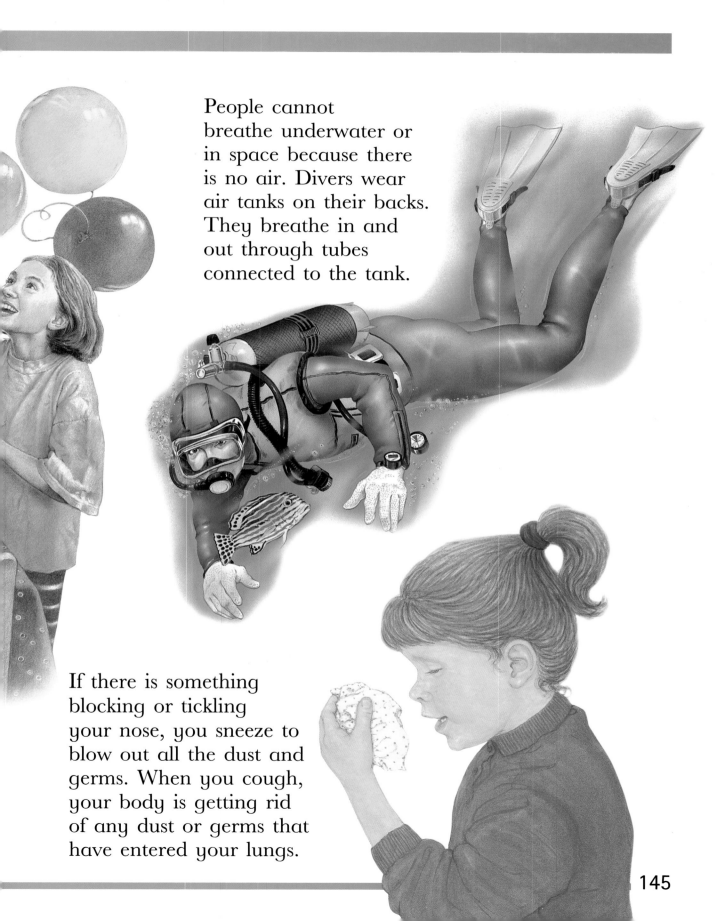

People cannot breathe underwater or in space because there is no air. Divers wear air tanks on their backs. They breathe in and out through tubes connected to the tank.

If there is something blocking or tickling your nose, you sneeze to blow out all the dust and germs. When you cough, your body is getting rid of any dust or germs that have entered your lungs.

The senses

You use your eyes, ears, nose, skin, and tongue to find out about the world around you. You look around and you listen, smell, touch, and taste things. You are using your five senses.

You feel things with your skin. The skin on fingertips is very sensitive. People who cannot see, "read" special raised text, called braille, with their fingertips.

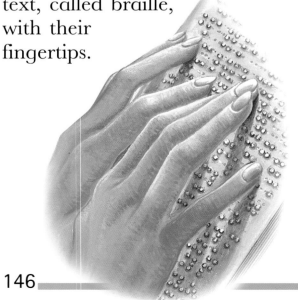

Think how hard it is to walk when you are blindfolded. Your eyes give you a lot of useful information. Your ears are able to pick up a huge range of sounds.

You taste things with your tongue, but your nose helps, too. It is hard to taste something properly unless you can smell it, too.

Smells float in the air and are picked up by your nose when you breathe in. You can tell the difference between thousands of different smells. Some things smell nice and others smell very bad.

Eating

The food you eat should give you all you need to live and grow. You need to eat many different kinds of food to stay strong and healthy, because they contain the different things that are important for your body.

Fresh fruits and vegetables are packed with vitamins and minerals, and other things your body needs.

Your body takes all the energy you need to work and play from your food. This is why you need to eat regular meals throughout the day.

Draw a chart like this on a big piece of paper. Then write down what you eat at each meal every day for a week. How many different types of food do you eat?

	Monday			
Tuesday			
Wednesday			
Thursday			
Friday			
Saturday			
Sunday			

Throat

After you swallow food, it travels down your throat to your stomach. It is turned into a mushy mass, then moves along your intestine. All the useful bits of food pass through the wall of your intestines into your blood.

Stomach

Small intestine

Large intestine

Babies

You started life no bigger than a dot in your mother's womb. You lived there for nine months, slowly growing until you looked like the baby shown here. Then, on your birthday, you were born and came out into a new world.

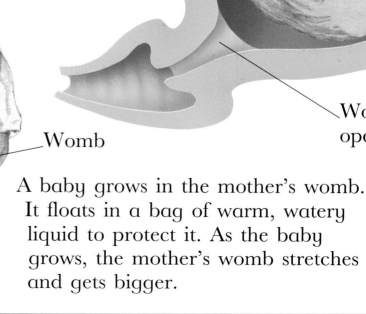

Womb

Womb opening

A baby grows in the mother's womb. It floats in a bag of warm, watery liquid to protect it. As the baby grows, the mother's womb stretches and gets bigger.

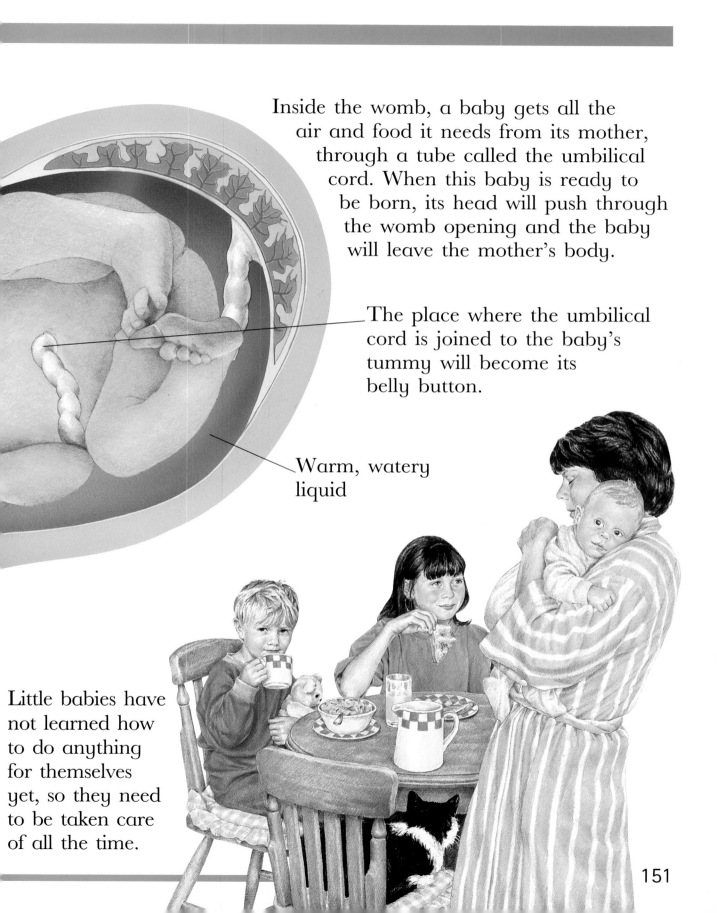

Inside the womb, a baby gets all the air and food it needs from its mother, through a tube called the umbilical cord. When this baby is ready to be born, its head will push through the womb opening and the baby will leave the mother's body.

The place where the umbilical cord is joined to the baby's tummy will become its belly button.

Warm, watery liquid

Little babies have not learned how to do anything for themselves yet, so they need to be taken care of all the time.

151

People and Places

Houses and homes

Around the world, people live in all kinds of different homes. They build them out of materials they find nearby. Some houses are made of bricks or stone. Others are made of wood, mud, or reeds.

Some people are nomads. This means that they move from place to place. These nomads in Mongolia live in round tents called "yurts."

People who live near rivers and marshes often build their houses on stilts, like this house in Indonesia. It is raised high above the ground, safe from flooding.

154

In North Africa, some houses are built of mud, with thick walls and small windows to keep out the sun.

MAKE A STILT HOUSE

Cut and fold back the ends of four cardboard tubes, as shown. Tape them to the bottom of a cardboard box. Fold a piece of cardboard in half and tape it to the box to make a roof. Paint doors and windows on the box. Glue drinking straws or popsicle sticks to the roof.

Apartment buildings, like this one in Africa, are built in cities where there is not much room to build. They let more people live in a smaller space.

This American house was built from bricks and wood. Both materials were easy to buy nearby.

Industry

Industries produce things that people need. Many industries make things, such as cars or buildings. Others produce the raw materials needed to make things, such as metal or oil.

The automobile industry produces cars. Billions of cars are made in factories every year. Most of them are put together on conveyor belts by robots.

Oil is needed to run machinery. There is oil buried under the ocean, so oil rigs are built on high platforms in the water. They drill deep into the seabed and pump the oil up to the surface.

Robot arm

Anchors hold oil platform in place

Helicopter
landing
pad

Crane

Drill

Many people work together to put up buildings. They use giant machines, like this crane, to lift huge pieces of buildings into place.

Scientists study chemicals. They figure out how to make medicines, plastics, and many other things that people use every day.

Religions

Many people around the world follow a religion. They believe in a god, or gods, who created the world and controls what happens in it. There are many religions. Each one has its own beliefs and traditions.

The religion of Jewish people is called Judaism. Jews believe in one god. They light candles in a special candlestick called a menorah during the festival of Hanukkah.

Hindus worship many different gods and believe that people's souls are born again after death. These women are celebrating Diwali, the festival of light. The god Shiva is shown on the left.

Muslims follow a religion called Islam, which was founded by the prophet Muhammad. They believe in a god called Allah, whom they worship in mosques. Their sacred book is called the Koran.

Minaret (tower) of a mosque

Christians worship one god and believe that Jesus Christ was his son. Their holy book is the Bible. They worship in churches, chapels, and cathedrals.

Church tower

Buddists follow the teachings of the Buddha, seen here, and worship in temples. They believe that people are born again after death and that good deeds are rewarded in the next life.

Festivals

Festivals are large celebrations with music, dancing, colorful costumes, and entertainment. Most festivals mark special days or events. Many are linked to a religion, while others may just celebrate the changing seasons.

Chinese people celebrate their New Year with a festival. Huge, brightly colored dragons lead processions through the streets. People carry lanterns and set off fireworks.

In Sweden, people decorate a pole and dance around it to celebrate Midsummer's Eve.

DECORATE SOME EGGS

Ask an adult to make small holes in the ends of some eggs. Blow out the insides, and rinse and dry the eggs. To paper an egg, paste small squares of paper all over it. To paint an egg, paint patterns on one half first. Let the paint dry, then paint the other half.

During the Japanese festival Hinamatsuri, people float paper flowers or dolls down a river to make their problems go away.

On Halloween, on October 31, people in the United States make spooky jack-o'-lanterns to scare away evil spirits.

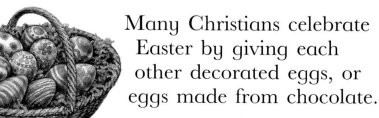

Many Christians celebrate Easter by giving each other decorated eggs, or eggs made from chocolate.

Trains, Boats, and Planes

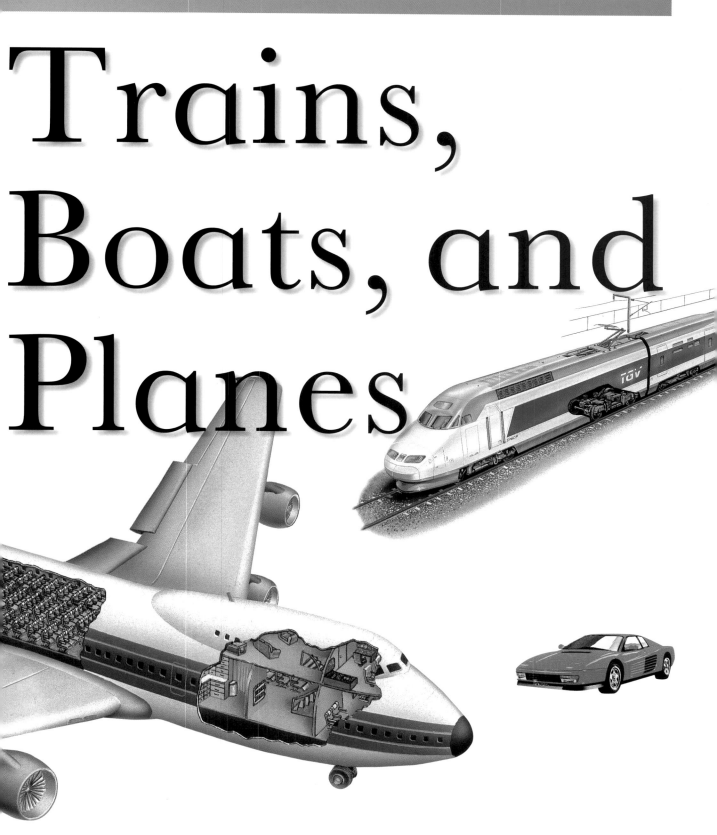

Tunnels and bridges

Tunnels and bridges make journeys shorter and easier. Bridges take roads and railroads over obstacles, such as rivers and highways. Tunnels are cut through mountains and under rivers and seas.

To build tunnels, people cut through the rock with giant tunneling machines, or blast huge holes using explosives.

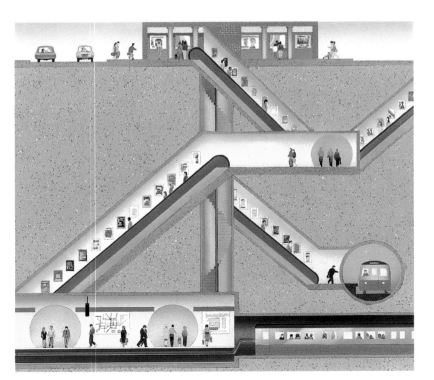

Subways are built in tunnels that run underneath big cities. Here you can see that different lines, going in different directions, are built at different depths.

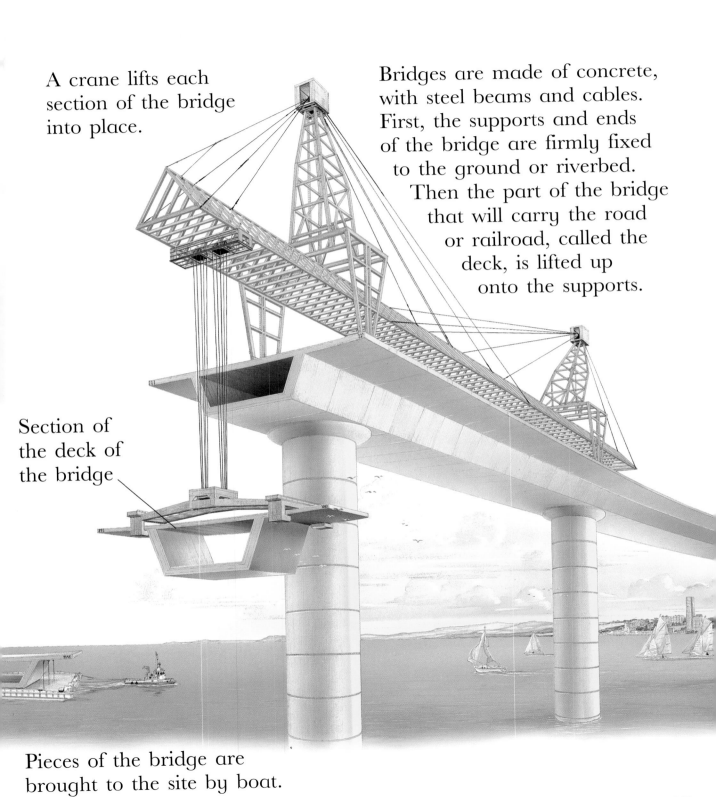

A crane lifts each section of the bridge into place.

Bridges are made of concrete, with steel beams and cables. First, the supports and ends of the bridge are firmly fixed to the ground or riverbed. Then the part of the bridge that will carry the road or railroad, called the deck, is lifted up onto the supports.

Section of the deck of the bridge

Pieces of the bridge are brought to the site by boat.

Submarines

Submarines can travel beneath the ocean for many weeks without coming up to the surface. Many submarines are underwater warships that carry missiles and other dangerous weapons. Others are used to explore the depths of the sea.

The first submarine used in warfare could only carry one person. He had to turn the propeller, steer the submarine to an enemy ship, and hook a bomb to its hull. This did not work, so the submarine was only used once.

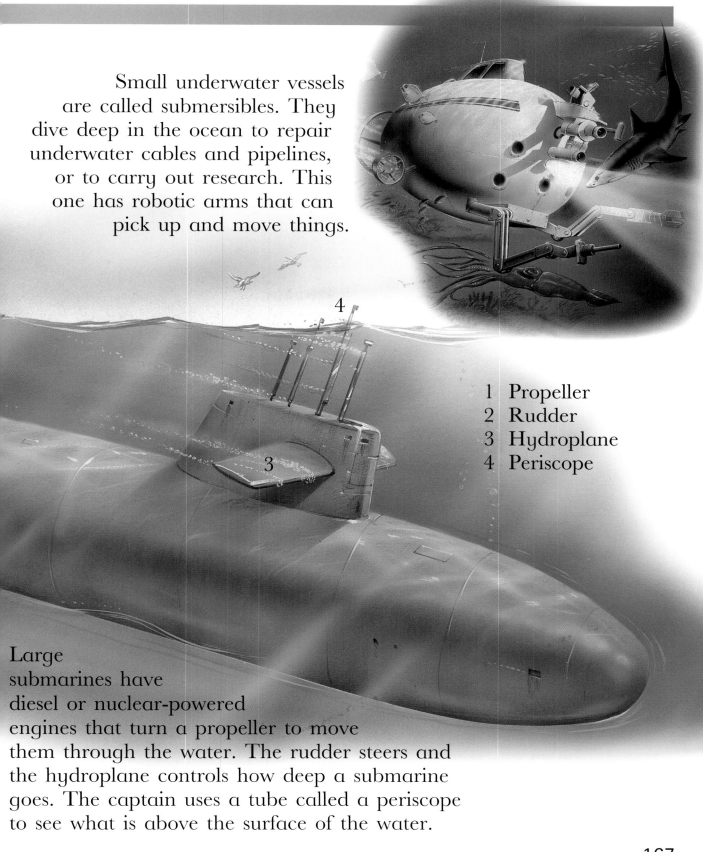

Small underwater vessels are called submersibles. They dive deep in the ocean to repair underwater cables and pipelines, or to carry out research. This one has robotic arms that can pick up and move things.

1 Propeller
2 Rudder
3 Hydroplane
4 Periscope

Large submarines have diesel or nuclear-powered engines that turn a propeller to move them through the water. The rudder steers and the hydroplane controls how deep a submarine goes. The captain uses a tube called a periscope to see what is above the surface of the water.

Traveling by air

Airliners are large airplanes with powerful jet engines. They can travel at speeds of more than 600 miles an hour. Airliners carry passengers great distances between countries very quickly.

This jumbo jet can carry over 400 passengers. The pilot and copilot who fly the plane sit in the flight deck.

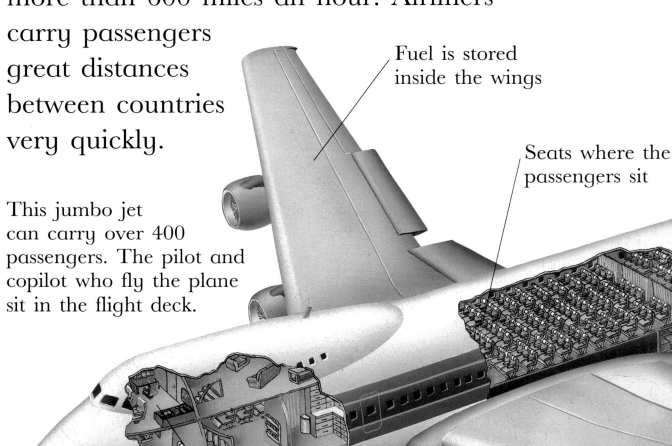

Fuel is stored inside the wings

Seats where the passengers sit

Jet engine

Flight deck

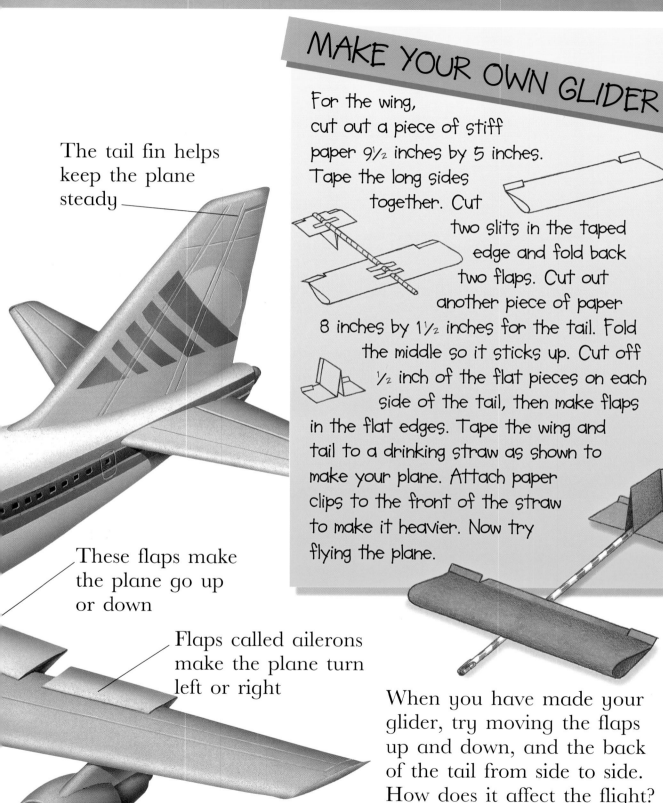

MAKE YOUR OWN GLIDER

The tail fin helps keep the plane steady

For the wing, cut out a piece of stiff paper 9½ inches by 5 inches. Tape the long sides together. Cut two slits in the taped edge and fold back two flaps. Cut out another piece of paper 8 inches by 1½ inches for the tail. Fold the middle so it sticks up. Cut off ½ inch of the flat pieces on each side of the tail, then make flaps in the flat edges. Tape the wing and tail to a drinking straw as shown to make your plane. Attach paper clips to the front of the straw to make it heavier. Now try flying the plane.

These flaps make the plane go up or down

Flaps called ailerons make the plane turn left or right

When you have made your glider, try moving the flaps up and down, and the back of the tail from side to side. How does it affect the flight?

Rescue vehicles

When there is an accident or a fire, special vehicles rush to the scene. They are specially equipped to rescue people and save buildings. The police, the fire department, and the ambulance service are the main emergency services.

The police use fast cars or bikes with sirens and flashing lights to reach the scene quickly.

Each emergency service does a different job. Ambulances rush injured people to the hospital for treatment. They have beds and medical equipment inside them. Trained staff lift people into the ambulance on stretchers and look after them until they arrive at the hospital.

Fire engines have extendable
ladders on turntables
that reach high
up buildings.

Fire fighters point
their powerful hoses
at the flames to
put out the fire.

How Things Work

What is it made of?

The things around you are not all made out of the same material. They are made from different materials, depending on what they are for. Materials can be soft, hard, heavy, light, rough, or smooth.

Do you know what your toys are made of? Soft things might be made of yarn or fabric. Smooth things can be made of metal, plastic, or glass.

Plastic

Fabric

Metal

Imitation fur

Paper

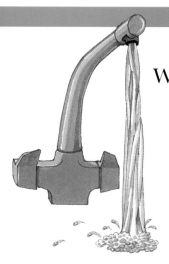

Water

Ice

Steam

Everything is either a liquid, a solid, or a gas. Liquids are runny. Solids have a fixed shape. Gases spread out to fill the space they are in. Some materials can change from one thing to another. Water is liquid, but when it freezes it turns into solid ice. If water boils, some of it becomes a gas called steam.

HOMEMADE POPSICLES

Pour your favorite fruit juice into a popsicle mold and put it in the freezer. When the popsicles are frozen, hold the mold under a warm tap for a few seconds, then gently slip them out of the mold.

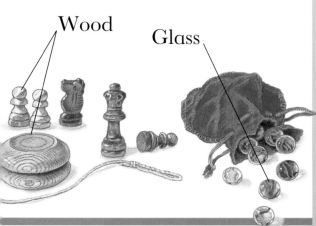

Wood

Glass

Hot and cold

Heat never stays in one place.
It moves around all the
time, spreading out
from warm places
to colder ones.
This is why hot
things cool down
and cold things
warm up.

Loose clothes let
air flow around the
body. People in hot
countries often wear
loose clothing to
keep cool.

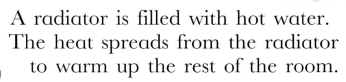

A radiator is filled with hot water.
The heat spreads from the radiator
to warm up the rest of the room.

It is very warm inside a greenhouse. The glass walls let the Sun's rays pass through them, but they do not let the heat escape.

The water in this metal saucepan is being heated on a stove. The heat passes from the stove to the saucepan and then to the water. Metal is used to make saucepans because heat travels through it very easily.

Light

Without light, we would not be able to see. Most of our light comes from the Sun. It travels through space very fast. Light is made by hot or burning things. Fires, light bulbs, and fireworks all make light.

The Moon cannot make its own light. The moonlight we see is really light from the Sun bouncing off the Moon. The Sun gives off light all the time, because it is a giant ball of burning gases.

MAKE SHADOW PUPPETS

Turn off the light in your room and ask a friend to shine a flashlight on the wall beside you. Put your hands between the flashlight and the wall, then hold them in these different positions to make animal shadows on the wall. Take turns holding the flashlight and making animal shadows.

Dog

Giraffe

Bird

When light hits a smooth, shiny surface, like this puddle, it bounces back again and you see a reflection.

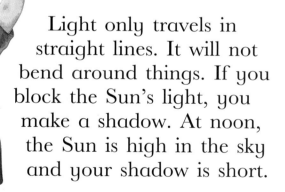

Light only travels in straight lines. It will not bend around things. If you block the Sun's light, you make a shadow. At noon, the Sun is high in the sky and your shadow is short.

Your shadow is always longer in the early morning or late afternoon.

Colors

Sunlight looks colorless, but in fact it is a mixture of different colors. You see all these colors in a rainbow, as the raindrops split the sunlight.

On a sunny day, you can make a rainbow with a hose. Stand with your back to the Sun and make a fine spray. You will see red, orange, yellow, green, blue, indigo, and violet.

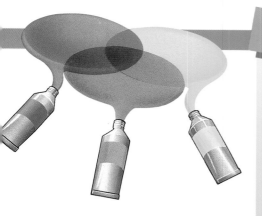

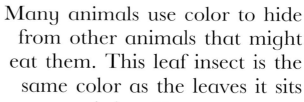

Draw glasses frames on a piece of cardboard. Copy a pair of glasses you have at home to make them the right size. Cut the glasses out and fold back the arms. Tape pink cellophane candy wrappers across the eyeholes on the back of the frames. Color and decorate the frames.

Blue, red, and yellow are called primary colors. By mixing them together, you can make most other colors except white.

Many animals use color to hide from other animals that might eat them. This leaf insect is the same color as the leaves it sits on, so it is hard to see.

The bright patterns on a butterfly's wings help it attract a mate. The blue eyespots also trick hungry hunters into thinking it is not a butterfly.

Sounds

There are sounds around us all the time—voices, music, traffic. Every sound you hear is made by something vibrating. This means that it is moving back and forth very quickly.

Sound can also travel through solid things. This boy can hear the girl banging the saucepan through the tabletop.

Sound moves through the air in waves. When someone speaks to you, they make vibrations in the air. The sound waves travel through the air to you. Your ears pick up the vibrations, and you hear sounds.

In a bottle organ, each bottle makes a different sound when you strike it. The more water there is in a bottle, the higher the sound it makes.

SEEING SOUNDS

You cannot see sound waves, but you can see their effects. Stretch some tinfoil tightly over a bowl. Fasten it with a rubber band to make a drum. Put some grains of uncooked rice on the drum, then bang a metal tray next to it. The sound waves will make the rice jump.

Sound travels four times faster through water than it does through air. It also travels much farther. Seals can hear each other underwater even when they are very far apart.

Movement

Movement uses energy, so all moving objects have to get the energy they need from somewhere. There are many different ways to do this.

Inside a vehicle, there is an engine that burns fuel, such as diesel oil or gas. When this fuel is burned, it releases energy that the vehicle uses to move.

Surfers use the ocean's energy to move. They wait for a big wave, then surf along it as it breaks. They are carried forward by the movement of the water.

You get energy from the food you eat. When you ride a bike, you use energy stored inside your body. You need to eat regularly so that you do not run out of energy.

Like all animals, these kangaroos get their energy from the food they eat.

You use your own energy to start a toboggan by giving it a push. When it is going downhill, the toboggan has enough energy to keep moving by itself.

Magnets

Magnets can pull—or attract—things toward them. Materials that are attracted to magnets are called magnetic. Most metals are magnetic, but paper, plastic, and wood are not.

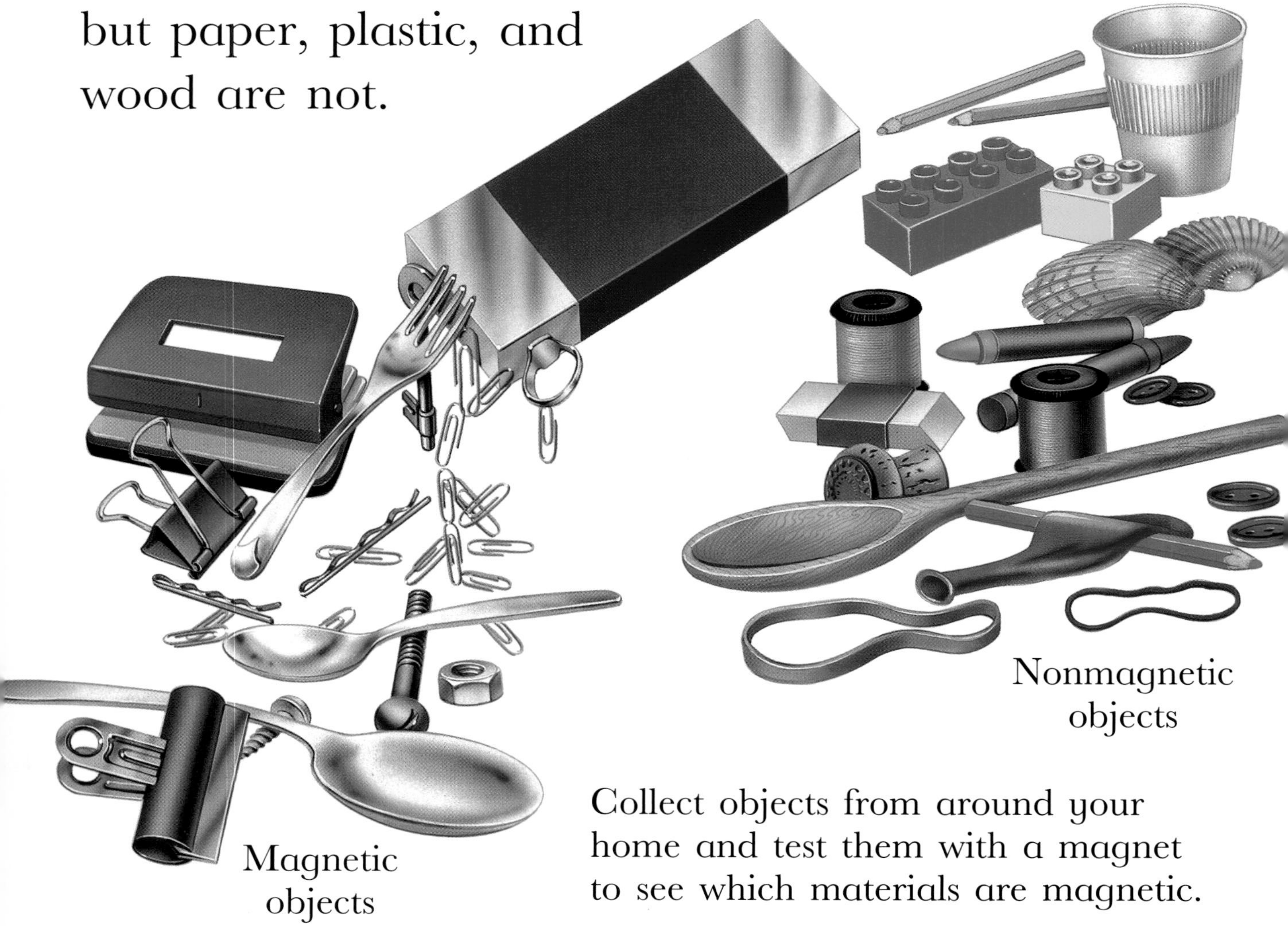

Nonmagnetic objects

Magnetic objects

Collect objects from around your home and test them with a magnet to see which materials are magnetic.

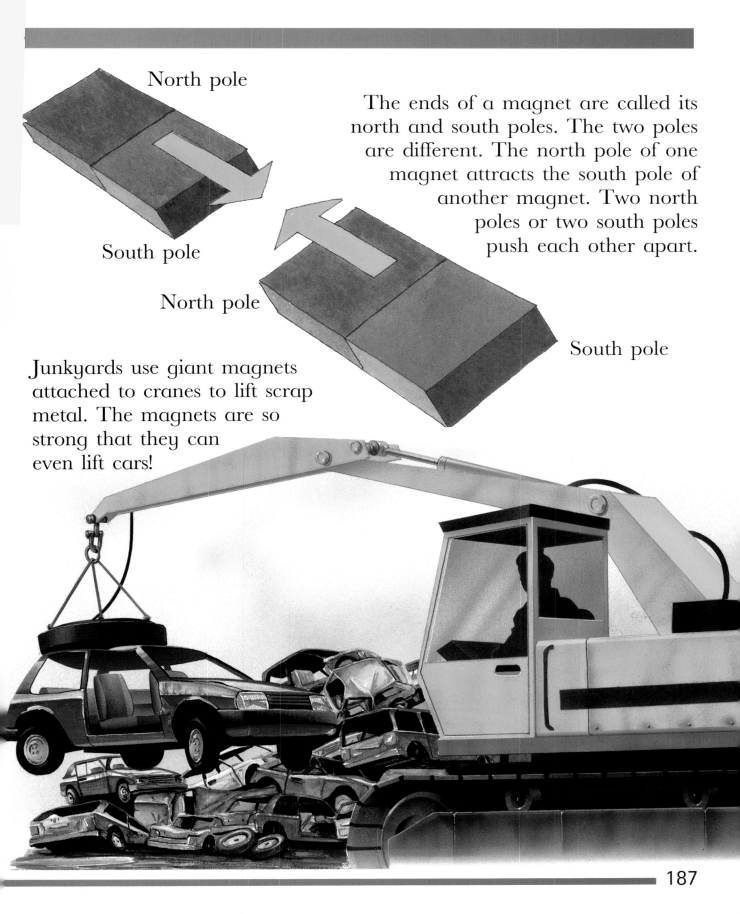

North pole

South pole

North pole

South pole

The ends of a magnet are called its north and south poles. The two poles are different. The north pole of one magnet attracts the south pole of another magnet. Two north poles or two south poles push each other apart.

Junkyards use giant magnets attached to cranes to lift scrap metal. The magnets are so strong that they can even lift cars!

Electricity

Electricity can be used to make heat and light and to power all kinds of machinery. It runs through all the wires in your home. Small amounts can also be stored in batteries.

This toaster runs on electricity. You can plug machines into the sockets around your home to make them work. Be careful when using electricity—you could get a dangerous electric shock.

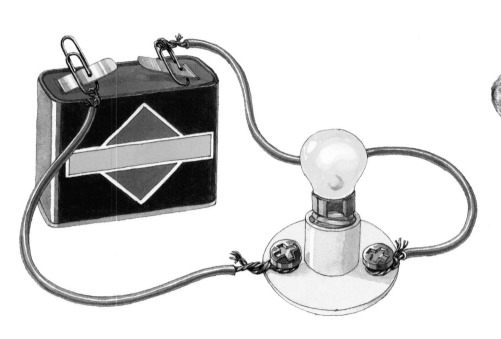

Electricity will only flow along wires if there are no gaps in the circuit. When the lightbulb is connected to the battery like this, the light will switch on.

MAKE A SIMPLE CIRCUIT

Screw a small bulb into a bulb holder. Take two pieces of electric wire and strip ½ inch of plastic from the ends of each. Attach one end of each piece of wire to a screw on the bulb holder. Attach paper clips to the other ends and clip them to the battery terminals.

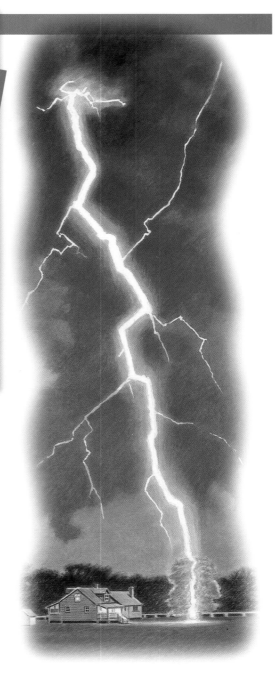

The lightning you see during a thunderstorm is electricity, but it is not the same as the electricity you use at home. Lightning is called static electricity.

Index

If you want to read about a subject, you can use this index to find out where it is in the book. It is in alphabetical order.

Acknowledgments

The publishers would like to thank the following artists for their contributions to this book:

Hemesh Alles, Marion Appleton, Mike Atkinson, Craig Austin, Julian Baker, Julie Banyard, John Barber, Andrew Beckett, Tim Beer, Richard Bonson, Derick Bown, Maggie Brand, Derek Brazell, Peter Bull, John Butler, Martin Camm, Jim Channel, Robin Carter, Adrian Chesterman, Dan Cole, Jeanne Colville, Tom Connell, Joanne Cowne, Peter Dennis, Sandra Doyle, Richard Draper, Brin Edwards, Colin Emberson, Diane Fawcett, James Field, Michael Fisher, Chris Fobey, Chris Forsey, Andrew French, Terence J. Gabbey, Peter Goodfellow, Ruby Green, Ray Grinaway, Terry Hadler, Nick Hawken, Tim Hayward, Karen Hiscock, David Holmes, Steve Holmes, Adam Hook, Christian Hook, Liza Horstman, Biz Hull, Mark Iley, Ian Jackson, Rob Jobson, Kevin Jones, Pete Kelly, Roger Kent, Tony Kenyon, David Kerney, Deborah Kindred, Steve Kirk, Mike Lacey, Stuart Lafford, Terence Lambert, Ruth Lindsay, Bernard Long, Chris Lyon, Kevin Maddison, Alan Male, Adam Marshall, Josephine Martin, David McAllister, Doreen McGuiness, Eva Melhuish, Steve Noon, Chris Orr, Nicki Palin, Darren Pattenden, Bruce Pearson, Liz Pepperell, Jane Pickering, Maurice Pledger, John Potter, Nigel Quigley, Sebastian Quigley, Elizabeth Rice, John Ridyard, John Rignall, Gordon Riley, Bernard Robinson, Eric Robinson, Eric Robson, Mike Roffe, David Russell, Mike Saunders, John Scory, Stephen Seymour, Rob Shone, Guy Smith, Clive Spong, Mark Stewart, Charlotte Stowell, Lucy Su, Treve Tamblin, Myke Taylor, Ian Thompson, Jean Paul Tibbles, Chris Turnball, Richard Ward, Ross Watton, Phil Weare, Rhian West James, Steve Weston, Lynne Willey, Ann Winterbotham, David Woods, Dan Wright, David Wright

Every effort has been made to credit the artists whose work appears in this book. The publishers apologize for any inadvertant omissions. We will be pleased to amend the acknowledgments in any future editions.